Date Due

NOV 12 1985	FEB 24 1995		
DEC 6 1985	APR 07 2000		
APR 29 1989			
JUL 02 1990			

Snukal, Sherman.
Talking dirty : a comedy of manners / by Sherman Snukal. -- Madeira Park, B.C. : Harbour Pub., 1983.
73 p. ; 28 cm.

02531453 ISBN: 0920080545 (pbk.) (w.o.)

I. Title.

TALKING DIRTY

Talking Dirty

A Comedy of Manners

By

Sherman Snukal

HARBOUR PUBLISHING
1983

COVER DESIGN AND PHOTOGRAPHS: Glen Erickson

TYPESETTING AND ASSEMBLY: Baseline Publication Trades Co-operative, Vancouver

PRINTING: First Folio Printing Co. Ltd. Vancouver

HARBOUR PUBLISHING CO. LTD.
Box 219, Madeira Park B.C. Canada V0N 2H0

PRINTED AND BOUND IN CANADA

To my mother and father

TALKING DIRTY was first presented by the Arts Club Theatre, Seymour Street, Vancouver, B.C. on October 13, 1981. The production was directed by Mario Crudo and designed by Douglas Welch with costumes by Linda Morgan and lighting by Marsha Sibthorpe. The stage manager was Louis-Marie Bournival. The cast was as follows:

MICHAEL	Norman Browning
DAVE	Dana Still
BETH	Sheelah Megill
KAREN	Gabrielle Rose
JACKIE	Alana Shields

Earlier drafts of TALKING DIRTY were developed with the help of the New Play Centre of Vancouver.

Scene I/about 12:30 Saturday afternoon
Scene II/about 9:30 that evening
Scene III/Sunday morning 11:30

TALKING DIRTY

The action takes place in Michael's apartment in the Kitsilano area of Vancouver.

TIME: The present. A weekend in May.

THE SET: A living room in an old house that has recently been reworked as a trendy apartment block. Lots of books, some plants, antiques, a Persian rug on the floor.

On the left, a door to the hall. Down right, a window looking out on to the street. Up right, the entrance to the dining room. At the back, off a small hall, the entrance to the kitchen and doors to the bedroom and bathroom. The kitchen and dining room are connected by an unseen passageway which allows free movement between the two rooms.

At the right, a large piece of antique furniture serves as a bar and also holds the stero equipment. A couch to the right of stage centre. A coffee table in front of the couch. A bonsai tree on the coffee table. To the left of the couch a small end table, lamp and comfortable armchair. A desk and bookcase at left.

Scene I

About 12:30 Saturday Afternoon

MICHAEL *is discovered sitting on the couch working. His notes and books are on the coffee table. After a moment he puts down his book and takes a sip of coffee. Then he turns on the stereo and, taking his coffee mug and a dirty ashtray, he enters the kitchen.*

There is a knock on the door.

MICHAEL *returns from the kitchen through the dining room entrance. He is carrying an open bottle of wine. He pours himself a glass of wine, moves a little to the music and sits down.*

There is another knock.

MICHAEL *turns off the stereo and answers the door.*

DAVE *is there. He is holding a small package.*

MICHAEL: Dave!

DAVE: Mike. How you doing?

MIKE *and* DAVE *give each other a hug.*

MICHAEL: *(pumping hands, slapping shoulders)* Jesus. It's been a while.

DAVE: No kidding.

MICHAEL: What are you doing here?

DAVE: I'm a conventioneer. Can you believe it?

MICHAEL: Come on in. When did you arrive?

DAVE: Last night.

MICHAEL: You should have called. I would have picked you up.

DAVE: Ah. Things were up in the air. I was going to go. And then I wasn't going to go. And then when I did go I had to take an afternoon flight, which means I arrived just in time to go to meetings all last night. I shouldn't be here right now. A thousand lawyers in the same room. The body rebels. The mind rebels. I was losing the ability to think.

MICHAEL: You've come to the right place. I haven't thought about anything in years. No Lynn and the kids?

DAVE: In Toronto. Minding the family estate.

MICHAEL *notices the box.* DAVE *waves it at him. Then he throws it to him.*

DAVE: For you. A new ball.

MICHAEL: Thanks. Never say die, eh Dave?

DAVE: I've been practicing. I've got a feeling that after twenty years I'm going to win the championship.

MICHAEL: Don't count your chickens. You want a drink?

DAVE: Sure. Mike.

DAVE *shows off his ensemble.*

MICHAEL: Very nice.

DAVE: Intelligent, successful, well dressed, but short.

MICHAEL: Not short Dave. Compact. More man per cubic inch.

DAVE: What counts in a man is density. Density and taste. *(showing the label)* Warren K. Cook. Top of the line.

MICHAEL: Very nice. Very lawyer.

DAVE: Mike.

DAVE *points to the floor*

MICHAEL: What?

DAVE *points again.*

MICHAEL: What?

DAVE: *(lifting his foot)* Pierre Cardin. One hundred and thirty dollars.

MICHAEL: *(lifting his foot)* Hudson's Bay. Forty-eight fifteen.

DAVE: On sale. Saved thirty bucks.

MICHAEL: Regular price. Includes tax.

MICHAEL *hands* DAVE *his drink.*

DAVE: Functional.

MICHAEL: You forget you have them on.

DAVE: Cheers. Not bad. *(noticing the notes)* Are you working this afternoon?

MICHAEL: Someone's coming over for a meeting but it's not for a while.

DAVE: By the way, your philosophy department made the Globe and Mail last week.

MICHAEL: Oh yeah.

DAVE: Something about the new head you got in January. He's some sort of hot shot?

MICHAEL: Kant scholar. Big jerk.

DAVE: You still making enemies of your department heads?

MICHAEL: What do you think? He hates my guts. I hate his. A very uncomplicated bit of social interaction. Thank God I've got tenure. Maybe I should have been a lawyer.

DAVE: Then you'd have partners. And they can also be a big pain in the ass. Such is life.

MICHAEL: I'll drink to that.

DAVE: I like the new place. How long has it been?

MICHAEL: A little over a month.

DAVE: Very academic. Hi yuh bonsai. Good to see you again. Don't worry about it. Short trees have more personality. Hey. Where's Beth?

There is a loud buzz from the kitchen.

MICHAEL: That's my oven. Saturday afternoon. Beth is probably shopping.

MICHAEL *enters the kitchen. He returns almost immediately.*

MICHAEL: *(perhaps just leaning his head out the door)* You want something?

DAVE: Nah. I just ate.

MICHAEL *returns to the kitchen.*

MICHAEL: *(off)* Where you staying?

DAVE: The Four Seasons.

MICHAEL: *(off)* Very nice.

DAVE: And the two dozen hookers on Georgia Street are that special touch that makes everything so much nicer.

MICHAEL: *(off)* A big tourist attraction.

DAVE: Yeah. I noticed the traffic jam taking in the sights.

MICHAEL *returns with his lunch.*

MICHAEL: Well, Dave, not that you're interested, but for a small fee you can take some of that scenery up to your room.

DAVE: What's that?

MICHAEL: Whole wheat bread. Crab meat. Edam cheese. Put it in your oven. Heat it up. Let the cheese melt. Voila. You sure?

DAVE: Nah. . Full. . Just a bite. . Not bad. Last night I watched three Japanese tourists purchase some of that scenery you were talking about. They bought six.

MICHAEL: Six?

DAVE: Six. The yen is strong. The dollar is weak. I'll have a little more.

MICHAEL: I could make you up one.

DAVE: Nah. Forget it. I'm not hungry. Mike. Do you ever wish you were Japanese?

MICHAEL: No. Do you?

DAVE: No. Yes. Lately I've been thinking it might make things a lot easier. Things are different over there. In the land of the rising sun.

MICHAEL: What are you talking about?

DAVE: I'm talking about geisha girls. I'm talking about the Liberal Party. I'm talking about feeling like the straightest married man in all of Ontario.

MICHAEL: What's bugging you?

DAVE: I don't know Mike. It's as though sex is some sort of perk. If you've been a lawyer for a while, if you've got a good reputation, if you're successful. Well then it only stands to reason that you join the Liberal Party and get a little something on the side. You remember my partner?

MICHAEL: Sure.

DAVE: Jim Bannerman and the Liberal Party are like this.

MICHAEL: You're not just talking politics are you?

DAVE: I see Jim every day. Lynn and I have dinner with him and his wife at least once a month. Their kids and our kids play hockey in our living room. Now get this. In March when we had that late blizzard and I had to get a room downtown, guess who and his girlfriend had a room just down the hall.

MICHAEL: Really?

DAVE: Really, really. I was going to be discreet and pretend I didn't see them but Bannerman ambles over and introduces me to his bimbo. Cool as a cucumber. Like they spent the evening playing Crazy Eights and eating popcorn. It's been going on for over two years. A very sophisticated liason. Every couple of months Bannerman and bimbo get away for a romantic weekend. This January it was Maui. Pretty nice for some people huh?

MICHAEL: I guess.

DAVE: I'm twice the lawyer he is. He's be out on the god damn street if it weren't for me. All the best accounts are mine. Everybody knows that. So, I've been thinking. This is Vancouver. Right?

MICHAEL: Right.

DAVE: And my home's in Toronto. Right?

MICHAEL: Right.

DAVE: So.

MICHAEL: So?

DAVE: So, I'm away.

MICHAEL: Away?

DAVE: Away from Lynn and the kids.

MICHAEL: Oh. Right.

DAVE: Yeah. Why the hell not? So that's what's been bugging me. Not very bright is it? What do you think?

MICHAEL: Look. I haven't been married for eight years but I know how it must be. If you feel you have to.

DAVE: I don't have to. I just want to.

MICHAEL: Well if you think it might be good for you.

DAVE: I don't think it will be good for me. It'll probably be terrible for me. What's the matter with you? You used to have an answer for everything.

MICHAEL: You know I understand.

DAVE: What do you mean 'understand'? I haven't done anything. There's nothing to understand.

MICHAEL: Well if you were to do something. Then I'd understand.

DAVE: Well I probably won't. I'm only thinking about it.

MICHAEL: It's your decision.

DAVE: I know it's my decision.

MICHAEL: I can't make your decision for you.

DAVE: I don't want you to make my decision for me. I want to know how you feel.

MICHAEL: It's not my place Dave. Look. I'm here. I'm your friend. Whatever you decide is fine with me.

DAVE: Terrific, wonderful, good friend. *(DAVE crosses to the bar, pours himself some wine)* Sorry Mike. You got any grass? I wouldn't mind some grass.

MICHAEL: Sure.

DAVE: I was just thinking out loud. My eighteen-year-old self got the best of me. Who am I kidding? Right? It's not me.

MICHAEL enters the dining room.

DAVE: *(more to himself)* Married eight years and you get an itch. The trick is not to scratch.

There is a knock on the door.

MICHAEL: *(off)* Will you get that Dave?

DAVE: Yeah.

DAVE answers the door. BETH is there. she is holding a cardboard box and a well-framed painting.

BETH: Dave.

DAVE: Beth.

BETH: When did you get in?

DAVE: Last night.

BETH: How are you?

DAVE: Great. Wonderful.

DAVE has by now put down his wine and helped BETH with the box and the painting. They hug each other.

DAVE: Cheap thrills.

BETH: Very nice.

DAVE: You look terrific.

BETH: And you look very prosperous.

DAVE: I am prosperous.

BETH: You're not all here.

DAVE: Only the neurotic half. I left the better half in Toronto. Lynn doesn't like conventions.

BETH: The legal one. At the Four Seasons?

DAVE: With the lawyers loitering in the Garden Lounge and the hookers loitering at the door.

BETH: Well, be good Dave. You're a lawyer. Not a travelling salesman.

DAVE: Ha ha.

BETH: A friend of mine was at the session this morning.

DAVE: Yeah? What's her name?

BETH: Earl Telford.

DAVE: Bright woman, taking a man's name in the legal profession. I'll say hello if I bump into him.

BETH: How are Lynn and the boys?

DAVE: She's great. Thin. She's running twenty miles a week. Dyed her hair. No, no. Rinsed it. She's going back to work in the fall. She's got kids. Now she wants money. The boys are almost human. I got Josh and Danny skating last winter. And Sean is talking and making a mess of everything. I think we spoil the shrimp rotten. How's Sir Frederic Banting?

BETH: It keeps me sane. I have grade nine this year. Lots of boys. All of them little savages. Are all fifteen-year-olds completely obsessed with sex? How were you at that age?

DAVE: I was great in crowds. I could bump into a different pair of breasts every five seconds.

MICHAEL *enters.*

MICHAEL: Hi honey. I thought I heard you.

MICHAEL *gives* BETH *a kiss.*

MICHAEL: What's all this?

BETH: It's yours. You left it when you moved. I thought you might want it back.

DAVE *stands up.*

MICHAEL: *(noticing* DAVE'S *reaction)* Yeah. Thanks. Isn't it great? Dave's going to be in town for a few days.

DAVE: Yup. Dave's in town. And in the dark.

BETH: There's another box in the car.

MICHAEL: I'll get it.

BETH: I can manage.

BETH exits.

DAVE: When did this happen?

MICHAEL: About six weeks ago.

DAVE: I just acted like an idiot in front of you.

MICHAEL: You didn't act like an idiot.

DAVE: Why didn't you tell me?

MICHAEL: You know how you get.

DAVE: What does that mean? How the hell do I get?

MICHAEL: Think.

DAVE: I'm a little irked that's all. What is it with you? Is three years the limit of your involvement with a woman? What are you, God's gift to women, that you have to spread yourself around? Make up your mind and settle down like the rest of the human race.

MICHAEL: I didn't see any sense in getting into this at long distance.

Short pause.

MICHAEL: Beth and I have been living together for over three years. We were thinking of buying a house together. And Beth needs a car. And I need dental work. And then there were going to be mortgage payments to make, for God knows how long. And then, of course, given all this mutual financial involvement and human nature, we'd get married and have kids. It's inevitable, isn't it? And then what would we be? Some sitcom in the suburbs. Me and Beth and Ginger and Skip and a big black lab that craps all over our back yard.

DAVE: Don't be so high and mighty. You're talking about my life. C'mon Mike. Any eighteen-year-old could give me that crap. You're thirty-three years old. Can't you do better than that?

MICHAEL: Every second Sunday we go to Beth's parents for dinner. Her Dad's this charming old jock who sits around drinking scotch and sneaking cigarettes and getting a little loaded and telling me about all the old boys on the rugby team and who died last week and how the market's going to do next week. After dinner, her mother, who is the nicest woman in the world but who talks too much and occasionally reminds me of Beth, which scares the shit right out of me, very graciously talks philosophy with me. Kahlil Gibran and Allan Watts and the meaning of life and also the meaning of marriage and just when are Beth and I going to make it legal. And it's warm and safe and snug in that living room with the fire in the hearth and the crocheted throws on the furniture and the After Eights in the china dish on the coffee table and all of us sitting around chatting like this wonderful family in the telephone commercials waiting for that long distance call from that other wonderful family sitting around the fire in Halifax. But Dave, from Sunday to Sunday nothing ever changes and it gets so warm and close in that living room that I feel like I can't move and if I don't get the hell out of there my life will be frozen in maple syrup forever.

DAVE: Why should you get away with it? You're not a kid. You grow old. Your life gets smaller. It's life. There's nothing anyone can do about it.

MICHAEL: You know my history with women. Nothing ever seems to last.

DAVE: I thought you felt differently about Beth.

MICHAEL: I do.

DAVE: So split. That's taking the bull by the horns.

MICHAEL: We haven't split up. Just because we no longer live together doesn't mean that we've split up. We've managed to work something out.

DAVE: Oh.

MICHAEL: Well there's always more than one way of looking at things isn't there? If you want to look at it in the worst possible light. Well. Then. Yes. We're both screwing around. But that's not the only way of looking at it.

DAVE: Uh-huh.

MICHAEL: I'm not denying there's sex. There's sex. There's always sex. It's a biological law. There's nothing anyone can do about it. But I don't think sex is central.

DAVE: Sure.

MICHAEL: Look, Dave, it was my idea. Okay? We have an arrangement. Some nights we see each other. Some nights we don't. We're playing it by ear. In another month or so a decision will be made.

DAVE: Can I say something?

MICHAEL: Shoot.

DAVE: Don't be a jerk.

MICHAEL: Wave your finger at me Dave. That's just what I need.

DAVE: And in the meantime you're single.

MICHAEL: In a manner of speaking.

DAVE: So how's the single life?

MICHAEL: I'm used to having Beth around. I'm on my own only I'm not really on my own. Some days I wake up by myself. Some days I wake up with Beth. Some days I wake up with someone else. It's confusing.

DAVE: Oh boo-hoo.

MICHAEL: I'm not complaining.

DAVE: Uh-huh. And?

MICHAEL: And?

DAVE: How's the sex?

MICHAEL: What do you want, the play by play?

DAVE: C'mon.

MICHAEL: Initially it was terrible. Christ I'd been with one woman for over three years.

DAVE: Yeah. I suppose. But you persevered?

MICHAEL: Yes. Of course. What did you want me to do? Give up?

DAVE: A good boy scout. And now?

MICHAEL: I'm doing all right.

DAVE: You're a great raconteur Mike. Anyone ever tell you that?

MICHAEL: What do you want Dave?

DAVE: Nothing. Just wondering if all single men find their sex life as boring.

MICHAEL: I'm not saying it's boring. It's not boring. Look Dave, I've been with one woman for over three years. During that time I've thought about other women. Who wouldn't? And some of these other women have thought about me. I know that. And now I have the opportunity to do something about what I've only been thinking about over these past three years.

DAVE: And all I'm asking is, how's it been?

MICHAEL: How do you think?

DAVE: What does Beth think of this arrangement?

MICHAEL: She had her reservations. But lately she's beginning to come around.

DAVE: You giving her in-class tests?

MICHAEL: She's enjoying her independence.

DAVE: Who's this Earl guy?

MICHAEL: Who?

DAVE: Earl Telford.

MICHAEL: Just a friend.

DAVE: You know him?

MICHAEL: We've never met. Beth met him swimming. Very buddy-buddy.

DAVE: But she has been seeing other guys?

MICHAEL: What do you mean 'seeing'?

DAVE: What do I mean 'away'?

MICHAEL: Yes.

DAVE: What do you think about it?

MICHAEL: I don't think about it.

DAVE: What do you mean 'you don't think about it'?

MICHAEL: *(intensely)* I mean I don't think about it.

DAVE: Oh. You don't think about it.

MICHAEL: What do you want me to do? Think about it? We have an arrangement. If I'm entitled, Beth's entitled. Why the hell should I let myself get upset?

BETH *enters carrying a box.*

BETH: Hello again.

MICHAEL *moves to help her.*

MICHAEL: Where'd you park? Burnaby?

BETH: I couldn't get the hatchback open. I had to drag this over the back seat.

DAVE: Michael just told me.

BETH: Yes.

DAVE: You look terrific.

BETH: What did you expect? A red mark on my cheek? My hair falling out in clumps?

DAVE: Ha ha. Very funny. Still have your sense of humour. I was just wondering how things are going.

BETH: Thanks for your concern. It's really not necessary.

DAVE: Good. So. You're having a great time?

MICHAEL: Dave.

BETH: Everything's fine Dave.

MICHAEL: That's all I said.

DAVE: You think you're typical?

BETH: What?

DAVE: There are some women . . . I mean I know some who wouldn't be so fine. They'd be full of hate and resentment.

BETH: Is something bothering you?

DAVE: Just wondering about human nature.

BETH: What about it?

DAVE: Maybe there's no such thing.

BETH: You're shocked by our behaviour, aren't you?

DAVE: Surprised that's all. You're both handling it so well. That's great. Good for you. But I've only seen you two as a couple. Never as an arrangement. And I'm a traditional guy. It's kind of confusing. I gotta go. They run the convention like a summer camp. If they don't see me for half an hour they'll have a search party out combing the woods. You free tonight Mike?

MICHAEL: For sure.

DAVE: Nine-thirty?

MICHAEL: Fine.

DAVE: Bye-bye Beth. Terrific.

MICHAEL: *(a pat on the back as he sees* DAVE *out the door)* See yuh buddy.

DAVE *leaves.*

BETH: Well? How was my performance?

MICHAEL: What?

BETH: Was I cool and casual enough? Do you think Dave was fooled?

MICHAEL: Beth.

BETH: What's bugging him? He seemed very . . . something.

MICHAEL: I just told him about us.

BETH: I know that. It seemed like something else . . . Oh. Never mind. It's probably me. Talking about our arrangement always makes me paranoid.

MICHAEL *throws* BETH *a look.*

BETH: Sorry.

MICHAEL: You're not paranoid.

BETH: Want to bet?

MICHAEL: Dave's away.

BETH: Away?

MICHAEL: He's thinking of getting laid. He's just thinking about it. He's probably won't do anything about it. Dave's always been terrible with women. I even had to get him together with his wife. Lynn was an old girlfriend of mine.

BETH: Weren't you generous? Did you offer my services this time around?

MICHAEL: I didn't mean it that way. In Dave's mind he's a sexual loser. A little fooling around may be good for him. A weekend affair. It happens all the time. What's the big deal?

BETH: Ask Lynn Mike. She may have the answer.

MICHAEL: Lynn doesn't have to know.

BETH: Was that what you told him?

MICHAEL: I didn't tell him anything. It's not my place. I'm Dave's friend. Whatever he does. I'm here. I understand . . . What would you have done?

BETH: Well if Dave was my best buddy and he's as happily

married as he seems, I would have tied him up until he got this silly idea out of his system.

MICHAEL: Right.

MICHAEL *gets up and walks towards the boxes. He takes a basketball from one of them and bounces it a few times.*

MICHAEL: Thanks for bringing all this stuff over. I was looking for this the other day. *(putting the basketball down)* What prompted all this?

BETH: I was cleaning up. It's not my stuff.

MICHAEL: *(picking up the painting)* I thought you liked this.

BETH: I do. But it's yours. I thought you'd like it back.

MICHAEL: Thanks.

MICHAEL *examines the wall. He jokingly places the painting against the door.*

MICHAEL: Here?

BETH *nods no.* MICHAEL *tries a few other areas.*

BETH: Better.

MICHAEL *enters the kitchen.*

BETH: You remember we're going to Ted and Anne's on Wednesday?

MICHAEL: *(off)* I've got it marked down. How's Ted doing?

BETH: Oh fine. Working hard.

MICHAEL: *(off)* He likes being a principal?

BETH: 'Like' is not the word. An intelligent career move as they say in the staff room.

MICHAEL *returns with a tool box.*

MICHAEL: We're not going to spend another evening listening to them ramble on about sailing. Their boat and their brass and their teak and their heads. *(mocking)* We've got two heads. Sleeps six. Had a lovely little sail up to Secret Cove. I wish to hell they'd stop talking about that boat and take us for a sail on the damn thing. How the hell can Ted afford it? What do they pay principals anyway? I don't know why I bothered getting a Ph.D. I should have gotten an M.Ed. and joined the Royal Vancouver Yacht Club.

BETH: It's a co-op. They own it with three other couples. And the only reason Ted and Anne went on about sailing was to prevent you from monopolizing the evening ranting and railing about first year students that can't read or write. Ted is a high school principal after all. I think he showed a lot of restraint.

MICHAEL: Oh. . Do I often embarrass you in public.?

BETH: You playing basketball at three?

MICHAEL: Term's over. No more games until the fall. Here?

BETH: You like your paintings on the ceiling?

MICHAEL: Karen's coming by. We're collaborating on a paper. Milton. How's this?

BETH: Eye level Mike.

MICHAEL: *(as he hands* BETH *the painting)* Oh. You do it.

BETH: What do you know about Milton?

MICHAEL: Nothing. Karen needed my background in transformational grammar.

BETH: Didn't that kind of paper go out of style years ago?

MICHAEL: Karen found an obscure journal that was interested. In the English Department one publication is as good as another. They don't read those articles. They just count them.

MICHAEL *takes a vase out of one of the boxes.*

MICHAEL: This isn't mine.

BETH: I wasn't sure.

MICHAEL: There's enough of this crap. Whose car did you borrow?

BETH: No one's. I bought one. It's just out front. The little red Rabbit. Now I can drive to Grandma's house.

MICHAEL: You didn't say anything.

BETH: Did I have to?

MICHAEL: No. Was that the down payment money.

BETH: Part of it.

MICHAEL: It's your money.

BETH: And I need a car. Besides it takes two incomes to buy a house these days.

MICHAEL: At least. . . It makes a hell of a lot of sense, Beth. Really.

Good luck with it. *(*MICHAEL *moves from the window to the bar and refills his glass.)* Want some? (BETH *shakes her head no.)* So. How does you little red Rabbit run?

BETH: It doesn't. It limps if I'm lucky. It won't start. And when it does it stalls. And then it won't start again.

MICHAEL: I'll take a look at it.

BETH: It's better now.

MICHAEL: It may happen again.

BETH: Actually I'm on my way to a friend's. He said he'd have a look at it.

MICHAEL: Didn't know Earl was so handy.

BETH: He feels responsible. He was the one who advised me to buy the car in the first place.

BETH *has now finished marking a place for the painting.* MICHAEL *picks up the hammer and moves toward the wall.*

MICHAEL: Well then it's only right that he should shoulder the blame If your little red Rabbit turns out to be little red lemon . . . You've been seeing a lot of Earl?

BETH: Yes.

MICHAEL: Still very buddy-buddy?

BETH: More than that.

MICHAEL *turns to the wall.*

MICHAEL: *(as he hammers in a hook)* Spatial relations isn't for me. I'm too logical. Derivations, completeness proofs, Goedel's theorem. That's my speed. Jigsaw puzzles on the other hand drive me crazy . . . Earl I'm sure will go far. I see the Liberal Party in his future. *(*MICHAEL *hangs the picture.)*

BETH: Mike. I don't think the picture is straight.

MICHAEL: *(letting it out)* Well what do you expect anyway? I'm a philosopher for Christ sake. Not a god damn interior decorator!

BETH *adjusts the picture.*

MICHAEL: Thanks for your help.

BETH: No charge . . Well I should be going.

MICHAEL: Why don't you join Dave and me tonight?

BETH: I'm sorry Mike. I've made other plans. Earl's throwing a party.

MICHAEL: Ah.

BETH *walks to the door.*

MICHAEL: Beth.

BETH: Yes.

MICHAEL: Don't forget your vase.

There is a knock on the door. KAREN *enters without waiting for* MICHAEL *to answer it.*

KAREN: I'm early. I know I'm early. You don't mind do you? *(sitting down, not waiting for a response)* Michael I've had a terrible day and I'm frazzled. Absolutely frazzled. *(taking off her shoes)* These shoes have got to go. Italian women must have the smallest feet in the world.

BETH: Hello Karen.

KAREN: Beth. Hello. How are you? I'm interrupting. I know I'm interrupting. I'm sorry. Truly sorry. Michael I'm leaving. Barefoot. These shoes will cripple me. Don't worry about me. I'll just pad up and down your hall.

MICHAEL: Relax.

BETH: I was just on my way out.

MICHAEL: Let me take your coat.

KAREN: *(handing her shoes to Beth)* Would you mind hanging it up? Raw silk. It cost me an arm and a leg. *(Michael takes the jacket. Karen takes her shoes from Beth)* And they say Italy is having financial difficulties. *(to Michael)* Thanks. We're working on this paper together. I need Michael's background in transformational grammar.

BETH: So Michael said.

KAREN: I'm *Paradise Lost.*

MICHAEL: *(picking up the tool box)* And I'm Past Participles. *(a soft shoe as he exits to the kitchen to put away the tool box)* You must have heard of us, the famous vaudeville team.

KAREN: Did I walk in at a bad time?

BETH: No.

KAREN: You sure? I can still make myself scarce.

BETH: I'm sure.

KAREN: Did you get that new racquet?

BETH: Oh damn it.

KAREN: You are coming tomorrow?

BETH: I'll be there. Where do you get the time for all your exercise?

KAREN: Do I exercise that much?

BETH: If you're not playing tennis you're playing squash. And if you're not squashing you're running in the rain just to clear your head.

KAREN: Well you're just as bad.

BETH: No I'm not.

KAREN: Well maybe so. But you don't need to. You're one of those lucky women. You're thin by nature. By nature I'm a tub. I was born fat and stayed fat for twenty years. Thank God for Weight Watchers and racquet sports. It's made my life bearable.

BETH: Karen we've been friends for years and you've never been anything other than thin. All you do is talk fat.

KAREN: Really? I talk about my weight a lot?

BETH: I'm sorry. I didn't mean it that way.

KAREN: Yes. Well. Weight-wise things are under control. And I guess generally things are moving forward.

MICHAEL *enters from the kitchen.*

KAREN: However, at present, as I was just saying to Michael, the shits. But I'll bore you with that tomorrow after our tennis lesson. Michael where did you get that hideous vase?

BETH: It's mine.

MICHAEL: She got it from me. It was a birthday present.

BETH: And I like it very much.

MICHAEL: And I know you do.

KAREN: Look at that. Two birds with one stone. Sorry. Sorry.

MICHAEL: Karen. How about some wine?

KAREN: Michael you are a life saver. Beth? How about you?

BETH: No. I really should be going.

MICHAEL *moves to the bar.* KAREN *moves to* BETH.

KAREN: *(an aside)* You know I play squash with Earl.

BETH: *(normal tone)* Yes. He says your game is improving.

KAREN: Thanks to him. We've become quite good friends. *(aside)* Very cute in white. Some women have all the luck.

BETH: Just what are you getting at?

KAREN: Nothing. Nothing. He is a lawyer though. I've always had this thing for lawyers. My father's a lawyer. *(*MICHAEL *approaches)* You look terrific. Have I told you that? *(taking the wine from* MICHAEL*)* Ah Michael. Thank you. *(a sip)* I must look a mess. Nice. I hope you've done your homework.

MICHAEL: Yes. And you?

KAREN: *(at her notes)* Busy little bee.

BETH: I'll leave you two to it.

KAREN: Why don't we go for brunch after tennis tomorrow?

BETH: Thanks. But I'm spending the afternoon with my parents. It's Mother's Day.

KAREN: Oh damn it. I'll be by that phone for an hour trying to get through.

BETH: Good luck with the paper. Don't forget Wednesday. Ted and Anne's.

MICHAEL: Right.

BETH *leaves.*

KAREN: I'm losing a friend.

MICHAEL: Don't be ridiculous.

KAREN: I know it. I'm losing a friend. I don't blame Beth. The way I behave around her I wouldn't like me either.

MICHAEL: What do you mean?

KAREN: Oh nothing. You know me. I get flustered and ramble on. Beth's certainly looking well. When I broke up with Danny I put on twenty pounds and my hair got so frizzy that I wore a scarf on my head for months. Stunning. Absolutely stunning. And it's only six weeks since you split up. She's certainly doing something right.

MICHAEL: *(at window, looking out)* We haven't split up.

KAREN: Whatever Michael. Whatever. What are you looking at out there?

MICHAEL: Beth's been having car trouble.

KAREN: *(crossing to window)* Oh she's fine. Peppy little thing, isn't it? Whose is it?

MICHAEL: Beth's. She bought it a few days ago.

KAREN: Oh. . With what? I thought every spare penny went for that house she wanted.

MICHAEL: Do you have those notes?

KAREN: Big step.

MICHAEL: You've been working hard.

KAREN: Beth forgot her vase. . It grows on you.

MICHAEL: Let's start with background material. Perhaps some very general information to put Milton and *Paradise Lost* in perspective.

KAREN: A little intellectual history.

MICHAEL: Right.

KAREN: For the Renaissance poets there were two major poetic forms: epic and tragedy. Milton divides the epic into two species: the diffuse epic in twelve books like *The Illiad* and *The Odyssey* and the brief type of which the *Book of Job* is the model. Could I have some more wine?

MICHAEL: Sure.

KAREN: I've had a terrible day. Melvin called from Whitehorse. He won't be coming down this weekend. Or any weekend for that matter. He's decided to spend his time entirely in the north.

MICHAEL: I'm sorry to hear that.

KAREN: I lost Melvin to the call of the wild. There's this teacher in Watson Lake. From what I gather Melvin heard her howling at the Arctic moon on more than one occasion but last night he succumbed and tracked her spoor across the frozen tundra. Now they're yelping together and I'm out in the cold. I'm writing the Territorial Council an anonymous letter about Melvin Preschuk, their flying dentist. I think he's made every white woman above the sixtieth parallel. To be perfectly honest Michael, the only reason I got serious with Melvin in the first place was because I thought, when you get right down to it, flying or not, a dentist is a dentist. Plodding, stable, middle-class and, I'll admit it, unthreatening and manageable. Was I wrong. I should have taken a chance on that attractive but sleazy Greek restaurateur . . . In high school I was the kind of girl who got firsts in everything but physics. I was never very attractive or popular. Too fat to be attractive. Too bright and bitchy to be popular. I think those miserable three years made me far too cautious about sexual matters.

MICHAEL: All of us feel, at one time or another, that we aren't as sexually adventurous as we had hoped.

KAREN: On the other hand, as you well know, I'm not a careful, conventional, introverted woman. I've been finding that the older I get the less discreet I become.

MICHAEL: And that's very admirable Karen. Trying to overcome your background that way.

KAREN: I know it sounds silly but it's been good for me. You should try it. It would be good for you. Oh I know you talk a good game Michael but really, deep down, you're very unadventurous.

MICHAEL: Oh am I?

KAREN: Don't be defensive.

MICHAEL: I'm not being defensive. I'm just trying to understand what you mean by 'sexually unadventurous'. Are you talking technique? What I do when I do it. Are you talking taste? Who I do it to and why. Or are you talking totals? How many I do it to and how often.

KAREN: I was talking timidity. And don't be such a philospher.

MICHAEL: So. There were two major poetic forms in the Renaissance. Epic and tragedy.

KAREN: Most Renaissance critics regard the epic as the greater form. This is the result of the epic's larger intellectual scope. Of course things have changed. I'm no longer an awkward, plain, teenager. I'm an attractive, successful career woman. Do you find me attractive?

MICHAEL: Of course I find you attractive.

KAREN: Don't humour me.

MICHAEL: I wasn't humouring you. You're very attractive.

KAREN: As an object of sexual desire?

MICHAEL: Only good breeding and an appreciation of high fashion prevents me from ripping the raw silk from your body.

KAREN: Thanks.

MICHAEL: Karen. We're friends.

KAREN: And you're a hypocrite. Last Christmas.

MICHAEL: You were missing Melvin. I was missing Beth. It was the festive season. We were just exchanging greetings. Besides, nothing happened.

KAREN: That faculty party.

MICHAEL: It was spring. The trees were budding. Everything was in blossom. More season's greetings. . . I was drinking brandy.

KAREN: Michael if that drunk, obnoxious, funny-looking man hadn't stumbled by . . .

MICHAEL: That drunk, obnoxious, funny-looking man just happens to be the pumpernickel head of the philosophy department and in his more lucid moments he is one of the world's foremost Kant scholars.

KAREN: You're very good at confusing the issue, aren't you?

MICHAEL: I think the most important thing for you to remember, in terms of this paper, is that a theory of transformational grammar must begin by making a fundamental distinction between linguistic competence and linguistic performance.

KAREN: You're a very reasonable man Michael.

MICHAEL: Well reason before passion don't you think?

KAREN: Not always. Sometimes it isn't reasonable to be reasonable. Sometimes we just have to say to hell with reason, to hell with obligation, I'm going to do what I damn well please and everything and everyone be damned!

MICHAEL: Linguistic performance is the actual use of language in concrete situations as opposed to linguistic competence which is the speaker's knowledge of his language.

KAREN: Arrangements like yours usually mean the end. They're the way decent, honest people fool themselves into thinking they still have something left. You and Beth have been making each other miserable for months.

MICHAEL: I was finding the relationship restrictive. I wanted more freedom.

KAREN: And now you have it.

MICHAEL: Yes.

KAREN: And Beth has it.

MICHAEL: Yes.

KAREN: And I have it.

MICHAEL *doesn't respond.*

KAREN: Okay . . We get along so wonderfully. I thought it would be a shame to waste it. When you really think about it, it does make so much sense . . Traditionally the epic begins at a low point in the middle of the action. For example, *The Odyssey* begins when Ulysses is farthest from home. In *Paradise Lost* the low point is the point farthest from God . . . Michael our friendship is something very special to me. I would hate for this little 'episode' to cause it any lasting damage . . . I'll read you some of this. You should have some idea how it sounds. 'Of man's first disobedience, and the fruit/of that forbidden tree whose mortal taste/ Brought death into the world, and all our woe . . . Well. Perhaps Milton said it all. I don't know what came over me. I'm really very, very sorry.

MICHAEL: *(standing up. During the course of this speech he will sit down on the couch beside* KAREN.*)* You're right. We do get along very well. And when you consider it dispassionately it makes a hell of a lot of sense. Now I'm not saying that we can say or do everything we want. That would be adolescent. On the other hand, the limits to personal freedom are a lot less strict than some people make out. And we should exercise that freedom, shouldn't we? To our own advantage. And what could the difficulties be? Especially if we're intelligent and educated and we try to be as frank and as candid as possible.

MICHAEL *kisses* KAREN. *She responds. While in the embrace* KAREN *moves the vase from the couch to the floor.*

THE LIGHTS FADE.

Scene II

About 9:30 that evening

MICHAEL *and* DAVE *are standing over a wastepaper basket at stage right.* DAVE *is holding a glass of wine.* MICHAEL'*s wine is on the desk at stage left.*

MICHAEL: I don't believe this. I really don't believe this.

DAVE: I don't care what you believe.

MICHAEL: I was in this room. I saw it. It went right in. Swoosh. And you're going to stand there and tell me, right to my face, that it bounced.

DAVE *takes a nerf ball from the waste paper basket.*

DAVE: It bounced. Bounce. And it doesn't count.

MICHAEL: Dave tell me. How did I miss it? How come you saw it bounce and I didn't? Was the sun in my eyes? Maybe it was the blonde in the stands? Or maybe this is all a bad dream? Maybe you're not here at all and I'm sitting at my desk reading?

DAVE: Don't give me your philosophy Mike.

MICHAEL: Okay Dave. Explain it to me.

DAVE: You blinked.

MICHAEL: Right.

DAVE: You blinked when it bounced. Everyone blinks. No complicated explanation.

MICHAEL: You're cheating Dave. You're cheating your best and oldest friend. And I'm disappointed in you as a friend and a human being. But I can see why you're a very successful lawyer.

DAVE *throws* MICHAEL *the nerf ball.*

DAVE: Take it over.

MICHAEL: I don't want to take it over. I want the point.

DAVE: Take the point.

MICHAEL: I don't need you to give me the point. I deserve the point.

DAVE: And it's yours if you want it.

MICHAEL: Well I don't want it. I won't take it over and I won't take the point.

DAVE: Take it over. That strikes me as a reasonable compromise.

MICHAEL: Forget it.

DAVE: Four one.

MICHAEL: Five one.

DAVE: Four one.

MICHAEL: It should have been six one. But we decided that since it's so difficult to decide whether the nerf ball bounces that it's five one.

MICHAEL *is about to throw.* DAVE *breaks his concentration.*

DAVE: What time does this thing start?

MICHAEL: I told you. Ten-thirty. All I could get were tickets for the second show.

MICHAEL *is about to throw.*

DAVE: Games to ten, right?

MICHAEL: Seven.

DAVE: Seven, right.

MICHAEL *hesitates.*

DAVE: Okay. Take your shot. You're delaying the game.

MICHAEL: Jesus.

MICHAEL *throws. He sinks it.*

DAVE: Fluke.

MICHAEL: You're a sweet guy Dave. Anyone ever tell you that?

They exchange places.

DAVE: Yeah. Lynn tells me that all the time. Okay Dave. Relax.

Don't think. Let the ball find the target.

DAVE *throws. He misses.*

DAVE: Shit. If this were Tokyo my life would be so much simpler. It would be stupid though. A wife, children, a family. To risk it all over a piece of ass. Idiotic.

MICHAEL *returns the ball.*

DAVE: Have I ever won at this?

MICHAEL: Once, nineteen sixty-eight. We were stoned on acid.

DAVE: That's right. I was a great acidhead. People loved me. Make me stupid and I'm everybody's friend. What is it? A buck a point?

MICHAEL: Two bucks a point and a five-dollar bonus to the winner. And it was your idea to play for money.

DAVE *throws. He misses.*

DAVE: I'll take it over.

MICHAEL: What?

DAVE: I'll take it over.

MICHAEL: Why?

DAVE: The music threw me off.

MICHAEL: What music?

DAVE: The music from the party down the hall.

MICHAEL: Dave.

DAVE: It's louder over here. And just as I was about to throw there was a sudden increase in volume and it threw me off.

MICHAEL: I didn't hear it.

DAVE: Well that stands to reason doesn't it?

MICHAEL: Why?

DAVE: Because if you can miss seeing a nerf ball bounce then you can sure as hell miss hearing a burst of music burst.

MICHAEL: What are you saying, Dave? That some time today I've had a cerebral hemorrhage?

DAVE: Okay. Okay. I'll take it over

MICHAEL *throws the ball back to* DAVE.

MICHAEL: Don't take it over. Take the point.

DAVE: No, no. I want to be fair. Don't be a big shot Mike. I only want what I deserve. You and Bannerman should get together. You've got a lot in common. You've both managed to work out very nice arrangements. Christ if Lynn had so much as an inkling that I'd been with another woman she'd be out on the town making the Maple Leafs to get even.

MICHAEL: Christ.

DAVE *throws. He sinks it.*

DAVE: Pretty good huh? I'll win this game yet. So three more shots this round.

MICHAEL: Two more. You've taken three.

DAVE: Yeah? Well, live and learn. You know who I've been thinking about all weekend? Brenda Lipton. The last of my single life. Well I went out in style. What the body of Brenda Lipton had that made it so unique was economy. Now don't get me wrong. I'm not talking petite. She was a big girl, was she not?

MICHAEL: Taller than me I think.

DAVE: Yeah. Tall and long. Just the way I like them.

MICHAEL: You and Paul Simon.

DAVE: Brenda was a wonderful girl, right?

MICHAEL: Right.

DAVE: Nothing but the essentials. An absolutely no-bullshit body. Long legs. Firm bum. Nice big boobs.

MICHAEL: Dave. Spare me.

DAVE: Mike. First of all I've got good taste and a way with words. And second of all you've got a present. All I've got is a past. She was a gymnast or a contortionist or something?

MICHAEL: A dancer.

DAVE: That's right. A dancer and double-jointed and she could do things I still remember. With her head facing one way and my head facing another.

MICHAEL: Like a Japanese woodcut. One time I put my back out.

Pause.

DAVE: I'd forgotten about that. But that's all right. Now I remember. You went out with her first. You set me up. You were a good friend. Like always. Thanks for reminding me. I appreciate it.

MICHAEL: I'm sorry. I thought you remembered. It seemed like that kind of conversation. It's your shot.

DAVE *drops the ball into the basket.*

DAVE: What do I owe you?

MICHAEL: Forget it.

DAVE: Don't tell me to forget it. What do I owe you?

MICHAEL: Eight bucks.

DAVE: And the bonus makes thirteen. Here's twenty. Go water your bonsai. *(waving his glass)* Any more?

MICHAEL: I'm out. How about a scotch.

DAVE: *(nods yes)* When does that show we're going to get out?

MICHAEL: I don't know. Midnight I guess.

DAVE: Let's not hang around. There's a party I'd like to catch.

MICHAEL: Sure.

DAVE: *(taking his drink from* MICHAEL*)* All I have is an address but I told some of the Vancouver guys I'd drop around to say goodbye.

MICHAEL: You don't like my scotch?

DAVE: I'd like soda.

MICHAEL: It doesn't need soda. Try it.

DAVE: I like my scotch with soda.

MICHAEL: I'm telling you it's Glenfiddich. It doesn't need soda. Just have it neat. If you don't like it I'll get you soda.

DAVE: Christ.

MICHAEL: Look Dave why ruin good liquor? If you're going to drown it in soda you might as well throw in Kool-Aid and drink it holding your nose. Just try it.

DAVE: And you don't judge. What is all this scotch business anyway? I don't like scotch. I've never liked scotch. Jim Bannerman drinks scotch. The Liberal Party drinks scotch. I'm a Canadian god damn it. I drink rye. And proud of it. It's good for every occasion. You want to drink cheap—

Five Star and ginger. You want to drink every day—C.C. and soda. And you want to drink special—Crown Royal on the rocks. Don't give me this Glenfiddich crap. No wonder this god damn country is falling apart!

DAVE *drinks.*

MICHAEL: Well?

DAVE: Where's your Kool-Aid?

MICHAEL: There's soda in the fridge.

DAVE *exits to the kitchen.*

MICHAEL: *(calling to* DAVE*)* I'm going to shave.

DAVE: *(off)* Yeah.

MICHAEL *exits to the bathroom.* DAVE *returns from the kitchen. He sits down and sips his drink. An electric razor is heard.* DAVE *glances at a magazine.* MICHAEL *wanders out of the bathroom with his cordless razor. He enters the bedroom to get a shirt then wanders into the living room to get some article of clothing from the living room closet. He returns to the bathroom.* DAVE *continues to skim his magazine. There is a knock on the door.* JACKIE *peeks in. She walks towards* DAVE.

JACKIE: Hello.

DAVE: Hello.

JACKIE: My name is Jacqueline LeMieux.

DAVE *extends his hand. They shake.*

DAVE: Dave Lerner.

JACKIE: Hi David. I'm a friend of Jim's. Jim Loadman? Blonde guy down the hall?

DAVE: Yeah?

JACKIE: Jim's throwing this huge party. Wall-to-wall people and it's only nine-thirty. Have we been disturbing you?

DAVE: Haven't heard a thing.

JACKIE: Listen. I don't know how to say this. This is going to sound strange no matter what. I'm a member of an organization called Kinergetics. Does the name Kinergetics ring a bell?

DAVE: No.

JACKIE: Kinergetics began here in Vancouver about two years ago and lately it's been really catching fire. Everybody's doing it.

DAVE: You selling something?

JACKIE: I can't believe this. You think Kinergetics is some sort of twisted religious cult?

DAVE: Something like that.

JACKIE: Very funny. It's actually very mainstream. Lots of professional people and people in the arts and media. Danny Simes? He's the film critic for the Sun.

DAVE: Never heard of him.

JACKIE: Suzie Brissenden? She's a sculptor. Had this show at that gallery on Pender Street. Some very unusual pieces.

DAVE: Actually I'm from out of town.

JACKIE: Becky Selig. She was with the Royal Winnipeg Ballet for ten years.

DAVE: I'm from Toronto.

JACKIE: Becky's the driving force behind Kinergetics.

DAVE: What's Kinergetics?

JACKIE: It's a movement place.

DAVE: A movement place?

JACKIE: People go there to move. By themselves. In couples. In groups. They move together. They touch each other. They relax. It's very therapeutic.

DAVE: Uh-huh.

JACKIE: Bernard Hedley. He's an older man, been painting for over forty years, kind of a mentor figure for me, well, he suggested I take it. Bernard thinks there's an intimate connection between body awareness and visual imagination. I think it's helping. Tuesday I went up like Baryshnikov and I came down like a DC-10. And tonight, just when I thought I was through with it, my back is killing me again. And, like I said, it's wall-to-wall people down the hall. So what I'm wondering is, can I lie down? I'll just be ten minutes.

DAVE: Sure. The bedroom's this way.

JACKIE: Now you're really going to think I'm a nut case. My

chiropractor recommended it. He's very progressive. And it's been written up in some very prestigious medical journals by some of the most famous orthopedic surgeons. I've sworn off beds. I use the floor.

DAVE: The floor?

JACKIE: Think about it for a minute. We spend a third of our life lying down. Why shouldn't lying posture be as important as standing posture? All I need is six square feet.

DAVE: Don't worry about it. Floor space is waste space.

DAVE *gestures to the floor.* JACKIE *sits.*

JACKIE: What's your name again?

DAVE: Dave Lerner.

JACKIE: I've always liked the name David.

DAVE: David and Goliath.

JACKIE: David Macfarlane. Do you know him?

DAVE: I don't think so.

JACKIE: Architect.

DAVE: Aah.

JACKIE: From Toronto. What do you do?

DAVE: I'm a lawyer.

JACKIE: Bill Maguire?

DAVE: Sorry.

JACKIE: He's my partner in movement class. Bill's a very sensual man as well as being a very successful lawyer. I don't think I've ever met a man with more eclectic tastes. Lawyer's are often surprising.

JACKIE *stretches out. Beat.*

JACKIE: Don't let me interrupt.

DAVE: No problem.

Beat.

DAVE: So? How do you like it down there?

JACKIE: It's a very comfortable rug.

DAVE: Persian. They're very comfortable.

JACKIE *exercises on the floor.*

DAVE: I've slept on the floor. In the past. I still do. Not as often as I'd like. You know how it is. You're a successful lawyer.

You get busy. You don't have time to sleep on the floor.

JACKIE: I've been thinking of giving up beds permanently.

JACKIE *exercises. Beat.*

DAVE: Designer jeans.

JACKIE: Calvin Klein.

DAVE: Aah. They fit well.

JACKIE: Size nine . . . Those are very unusual shoes.

DAVE: You think so? Pierre Cardin.

JACKIE: Very nice.

DAVE: *(showing his foot)* Size eight-and-a-half D.

JACKIE *giggles.* MICHAEL *enters.*

DAVE: Ah Mike. Jackie, this is my buddy Michael Kaye. This is his place. Mike this is the lovely and charming Jacqueline LeMieux.

JACKIE: Hello.

MICHAEL: Hi.

DAVE: Jackie was at a party just down the hall. She has a bad back but there was no place to lie down there. So she's going to use your floor for a while.

MICHAEL: Sure. What's the problem?

JACKIE: Muscle inflammation. Lumbar region. It needs support. I strained it at Kinergetics. That's a movement place. People go there to move.

MICHAEL: Uh-huh.

JACKIE: I'll just be ten minutes.

MICHAEL: That's fine. Will you excuse us?

DAVE: We'll just be a sec Jackie.

MICHAEL *and* DAVE *move away from* JACKIE.

MICHAEL: What's she doing here?

DAVE: Don't worry about it.

MICHAEL: We're going out.

DAVE: We've got lots of time. The woman is in a lot of pain.

MICHAEL: Why on my living room rug?

DAVE: Why not? She helps the décor.

JACKIE: *(calling to* MICHAEL*)* I like your art.

MICHAEL: *(turning)* What?

JACKIE: Is that a Dondell?

MICHAEL: That's right.

JACKIE: It must be one of Jack's older pieces. What do you do Michael?

MICHAEL: I teach philosophy at UBC.

JACKIE: Aesthetics is my interest. What's your field?

MICHAEL: Philosophy of language.

JACKIE: Words and things.

MICHAEL: In a manner of speaking.

DAVE: And you Jackie? What do you do for a living?

JACKIE: I paint. So I notice good art when I see it.

DAVE: Have you had any shows?

JACKIE: I'm just starting out.

DAVE: I've got a friend who's an artist. It's a tough life. Only the very best make a living at it.

JACKIE: Money's not everything. Besides I'm optimistic.

MICHAEL: That's the spirit.

JACKIE: Hope springs eternal.

MICHAEL: You can't rush these things.

JACKIE: You shouldn't

MICHAEL: It's all developmental.

JACKIE: A slow painful process. Ow.

MICHAEL: What is it?

JACKIE: Muscle spasm.

MICHAEL: Oh. Can I get you something?

JACKIE: I have some Darvon at Jim's but I've taken a few already. I'll just have to grin and bear it . . . There is something. Can you pop my back? My chiropractor does it. It sets me up for hours.

MICHAEL: Ah . . Yeah . . Well . . Sure . . I've never done this before. Uh. What do I have to do?

DAVE: Actually. And I don't want to brag. I have loads of experience.

MICHAEL: That's all right Dave.

JACKIE *turns on her stomach.*

JACKIE: Kneel down. One leg on either side of me.

MICHAEL: Yes.

JACKIE: Place your hands really low on my back.

MICHAEL: Really low?

JACKIE: That's right.

MICHAEL: This okay?

JACKIE: Lower.

MICHAEL *hesitates.*

DAVE: You want me to do it?

MICHAEL: I've got it.

JACKIE: Now make sure your hands are on either side of my backbone.

MICHAEL: It's hard to find you backbone way down here.

DAVE: I'll show you. Right here.

MICHAEL: Forget it Dave.

JACKIE: Now, with the insides of your wrists facing each other and your fingers spread, lean forward with all your might.

MICHAEL: Hang on a second.

DAVE: *(showing* MICHAEL *the hand position)* Like this.

MICHAEL: Dave. Now what?

JACKIE: Just put your weight on your hands and lean forward.

MICHAEL *attempts it awkwardly.*

MICHAEL: How's that?

JACKIE: Not good.

DAVE: Let me try.

JACKIE: *(to* DAVE*)* That's all right. It helped a little.

DAVE: So Jackie, where would you be on this Saturday night if you weren't lying on the floor?

JACKIE: I'm at a party. Jim's. Just down the hall.

DAVE: Oh. Right. Sorry.

JACKIE: I usually work Saturday nights.

DAVE: No kidding? You paint away your Saturday nights. Art's important Jackie. But all work and no play.

JACKIE: I'm a cocktail waitress.

DAVE: That's interesting. Where do you work?

JACKIE: Creole Pete's.

DAVE: I don't know it.

MICHAEL: Their chicken gumbo is out of this world.

JACKIE: There's nothing like it.

DAVE: It must be a demanding job being a cocktail waitress.

JACKIE: It's all right.

MICHAEL: It gets an interesting crowd.

JACKIE: That's the best thing about it. Meeting all those unusual people.

DAVE: How do you do it? There must be a trick to it. Keeping all those glasses and bottles upright on your tray, not spilling a drop, threading your way through a crowded room.

JACKIE: No problem.

MICHAEL: Funny. I've never seen you there.

JACKIE: I think I've seen you around.

MICHAEL: Really?

JACKIE: Yes. I think so.

MICHAEL: You do look kind of familiar now that I think about it.

DAVE: Do you hold your tray like this? Or like this?

MICHAEL: You looking for work Dave? I usually eat there on Wednesdays.

JACKIE: I have the section near the windows.

MICHAEL: I'll look for you.

DAVE: Mike. Get the lady a drink. Be a good host. You want a drink, don't you Jackie?

JACKIE: *(to* DAVE*)* I wouldn't mind some water. Perrier? With a twist?

MICHAEL: *(after* DAVE *refuses to move)* Coming up. Excuse me Jackie.

MICHAEL *enters the kitchen.* JACKIE *exercises.*

DAVE: Jackie. . .

JACKIE: Yes.

DAVE: It's Saturday night. I was thinking. . .

JACKIE: Do you know that evolutionarily speaking the backbone is the oldest bone we have?

DAVE: Jackie listen.

DAVE *hesitates.*

JACKIE: Yes.

DAVE: I'm away.

JACKIE: What?

DAVE: What I mean is, I live in Toronto. Did I tell you that?

JACKIE: Uh-huh. Do you travel a lot?

DAVE: Uh. Yeah.

JACKIE: That's a big dream of mine. To have the time and the money to just travel.

DAVE: I've been around. All over the world. One day Toronto. The next Vancouver, L.A., New York. Last week I was in London. That's the kind of practice I have. Lots of multi-nationals. And right now. Like I was saying. I'm not in Toronto. I'm away.

JACKIE: I've been to Toronto.

DAVE: Great town. No place like it in the world. And I've seen them all.

JACKIE: It's not my kind of city. All that concrete and cars and people. I like Vancouver with the mountains and the vistas and the natural grandeur.

DAVE: You're right there. You sure as hell don't get your mountains and your vistas and your natural grandeur on the corner of Bloor and Bathurst. My wife always complains about that. . . .

JACKIE: You're married?

DAVE: Yeah. Married. Eight years. Three boys.

JACKIE: That's nice.

DAVE: Yeah. Terrific.

MICHAEL *enters with Perrier.*

MICHAEL: Here we go.

JACKIE: Thanks.

MICHAEL: I'm sorry. Can I offer you something to eat?

JACKIE: No thanks. I'm watching my weight.

DAVE: *(mocking, anger)* Calvin Klein. Size nine.

DAVE *exits to the dining room.*

MICHAEL: What was all that about?

JACKIE: Your friend's married. He lives in Toronto. With his wife and three kids. He's away.

MICHAEL: Shit!

DAVE *enters.*

MICHAEL: Dave.

DAVE: Where are those joints?

MICHAEL: Dave.

DAVE: Where are those joints?

MICHAEL: Right hand drawer.

DAVE *returns to the dining room.*

JACKIE: He made his move as soon as you left.

MICHAEL: *(just a look)*

JACKIE: You're not married are you?

MICHAEL: No.

JACKIE: I didn't think so. You don't have the ambiance.

MICHAEL: Look Jackie. Things are getting a little complicated. . Maybe you should . . .

JACKIE: I like your place Michael. It makes its statement. Sophisticated, intelligent but not uptight.

JACKIE *opens the door to the bedroom and peeks in.*

MICHAEL: Jackie.

DAVE: *(off, loudly, perhaps slamming a drawer)* Matches!

There is a knock on the door.

MICHAEL: What?

MICHAEL *answers it.* BETH *strides into the living room.*

BETH: Hello.

MICHAEL: Hello.

JACKIE: Hello.

MICHAEL: Oh. Beth. This is Jackie uh . . .

JACKIE: LeMieux.

MICHAEL: LeMieux. Jackie this is Beth Gordon.

JACKIE: Hi.

BETH: Hello.

JACKIE *lies down on the rug.*

MICHAEL: Jackie has a bad back. I just met Jackie ten minutes ago. She was at a party down the hall. She needs a place to lie down. Dave and I were just on our way out. He's in the dining room toking up.

DAVE: *(off)* Where are those goddamn matches?

MICHAEL: See. . Well. . How's the car?

BETH: No better. Stall, start, stall, start. It stalled just now and I couldn't get it started. I'm amazed I get anywhere at all.

MICHAEL: You should speak to your dealer about that car.

BETH: Either I get a replacement or they return my money.

MICHAEL: Exactly.

BETH: If only I could run my life on that straightforward a basis.

MICHAEL: Jackie would you mind?

JACKIE *begins to get up.*

BETH: What is it Michael? Do you think I'll embarrass you in front of your guests?

JACKIE *lies back down.*

BETH: I just came from my parents'.

MICHAEL: Ah. How are they?

BETH: Mother invited me over for 'tea.'

MICHAEL: Right.

BETH: Yes. Well I haven't seen very much of her lately. It wasn't very pleasant. I told mother not to worry. You and I just needed some time to work the kinks out of our relationship. Mother replied that she and father have been happily married for over thirty years and they never once used the word 'relationship'. I said times had changed. People aren't the same. Pressures are very different. We have an arrangement. We're going to work things out. 'Arrangement' bothered mother. She said that in her opinion, except for it musical use, the term 'arrangement' shouldn't be used in polite society. She asked me if it was one of your words. I said it was.

MICHAEL: Do you want me to give her a call?

BETH: No. She doesn't want to talk to you. She wants to wash your mouth out with soap.

MICHAEL: Jackie.

JACKIE *gets up, takes her glass of Perrier, heads for the hall then, remembering her glass, enters the kitchen.*

BETH: Actually, to be honest, in spite of everything, she seems to have a fondness for you. She invited you to dinner tomorrow night. I said you couldn't make it.

MICHAEL: Why?

BETH: Because I didn't want to sit around the table with my family, on Mother's Day, in the house where I grew up and pretend that everything is hunky-dory between you and me knowing all the while that I'm seeing you and Earl and you're seeing me and God knows how many other women. I haven't felt as guilty since I was eighteen and hiding my pills and lying to my parents about just what I was doing out until four in the morning. Jesus Christ I'm thirty years old and I feel like a teenager. I don't know what I'm doing. Half the time I don't know whether to laugh or cry. This god damn arrangement. Smiling at each other and pretending we're these sophisticated, enlightened people. It makes me nauseous.

MICHAEL: I thought we decided not to have this conversation.

BETH: You decided. I capitulated.

MICHAEL: I seem to remember it as a mutual agreement! . . . Beth. There's no point in rehashing things. Talking about it only makes us both upset.

BETH: Talking about it makes me upset . . It's just another philosophical conversation to you.

MICHAEL: Now is not the time.

BETH: I don't know how you can live like this. Sweeping everything under the rug. What is it with you? The only position you're happy in is sitting on the fence.

MICHAEL: Okay, okay. Let's talk.

BETH: I don't want to talk. I want to scream and yell and break things over your head.

MICHAEL: That won't solve anything.

BETH: It will make me feel a hell of a lot better.

MICHAEL: Beth, what is it you want from me.

BETH: I love you. I want you to make up your god damn mind.

DAVE *enters with an unlit joint and matches.*

DAVE: Hi Beth. Do you want some of this?

BETH: No thanks.

DAVE: Mike?

MICHAEL: No.

DAVE: *(holding* BETH*'s hand)* How are you doing? You're looking terrific. As usual.

BETH: Thanks Dave.

DAVE: Why don't you join us tonight?

BETH: I'm sorry but I have other plans.

DAVE: That's too bad. It would have been nice to spend some time with you.

BETH: Thank you Dave. I appreciate that. *(*BETH *crosses to the door then moves to the desk.)* May I use your phone?

MICHAEL: Of course.

BETH *looks through the yellow pages.*

MICHAEL: You looking for anything in particular?

BETH: I'm calling a cab.

MICHAEL: Take my car. We don't need it.

BETH: No.

MICHAEL: Why not?

BETH: I don't want it.

MICHAEL: Okay, okay. Let me look at your car.

BETH: I don't need your help.

MICHAEL: Beth please. This isn't doing any good. I don't have to see Dave tonight. He'll understand. You and I can have that talk.

BETH: Why bother Michael? You'll put things off and I'll give in. We're not the best of people are we? You're scared and I'm weak. But that's who we are. We might as well make the best of it.

BETH *looks through the phone book.* MICHAEL *crosses to* DAVE *who is at extreme stage right.*

MICHAEL: Give her a hand.

DAVE: *(as* MICHAEL *moves him across the stage)* What?

MICHAEL: Give her a hand with the car.

DAVE: I don't know anything about cars.

MICHAEL: *(taking the phone from* BETH *and hanging it up)* Dave will give you a hand.

DAVE: I'll have you going in no time.

BETH *leaves. Dave shrugs his shoulders at* MICHAEL.

MICHAEL: Just try will you?

DAVE *leaves.* MICHAEL *sits down on the couch. Then he walks to the window.* JACKIE *enters from the kitchen with her Perrier.* MICHAEL *doesn't notice her.*

JACKIE: Resentment, resentment, resentment.

MICHAEL: What?

JACKIE: Resentment. Your ex-girlfriend's reaction. You can't let it get you down. We do what we have to do. If people resent and can't forgive. That's too bad for them. We just have to accept it as one of the consequences of doing what we want to do.

MICHAEL: Jackie. I'd really like to be alone.

JACKIE: Jeffrey Fiskin. Psychiatrist. Very eclectic. Jung. Freud. Theatre games. Body work. Once he made me listen to *Blonde on Blonde* for an entire afternoon. When's the last time you spent four hours listening to *Blonde on Blonde?* Jeffrey Fiskin is a very perceptive man. I recommend him wholeheartedly.

MICHAEL: Jackie. I don't know you. You've been lying on my living room floor for the last half hour. I just had a falling out with my best buddy over your lumbar region. You saw what happened between me and my girlfriend or whatever she is. And Bob Dylan is forty-three years old. Now don't you think it's time for you to leave?

JACKIE: I throw up. Every couple of weeks. Things are going along smoothly. Then. All of a sudden. Vomit. I'm sweating. I can hardly move. I feel like I'm going to die. Jeffrey says it's a hysterical reaction. He says I'm still trying to deal with Burnaby . . . Environmentally I was being under-stimulated. Artistically I was being under-utilized. Intellectually I was being under-exercised. But you must have heard it all before. It's the same old story. I was born there. And I went to school there. And I met a guy there. And I was going to raise a family there. And then it hit me. I was going to live and die knowing only Burnaby. But Burnaby's not me. And I'm not Burnaby. So now, every couple of weeks or so, when Burnaby rears its ugly head, I throw up and feel like I'm going to die.

JACKIE *stifles a belch.*

MICHAEL: You're not going to throw up now are you?

JACKIE: I'm not going to throw up. I haven't felt as good in months. Too much Perrier water. Can I use your bathroom?

JACKIE *enters the bathroom without waiting for* MICHAEL *to repond.* MICHAEL *walks to the window and looks out. There is a knock on the door.* KAREN *sticks her head into the apartment.*

KAREN: Hello.

MICHAEL: Karen. Hello.

KAREN *enters the apartment. She is carrying a bouquet of flowers and a bottle of wine.*

KAREN: I was driving by and I saw the light.

MICHAEL *notices the flowers and wine.*

KAREN: Well. To be frank. I bought the flowers and the wine first. I was hoping you'd be home. And luck was with me. Narcissus. It's all over for the tulips and the daffodils. Nice. Aren't they? I stole them. Figuratively. There's this Chinese grocery on South Granville that has the freshest flowers and the cheapest prices.

KAREN *offers the flowers to* MICHAEL.

MICHAEL: Thank you.

KAREN: You know me and sexual stereotyping. The talk of the English Department. A full-bodied red with a pleasing bouquet. Also politically correct. From the now-socialist France. Also, as French wines go, very cheap.

KAREN *offers the wine.*

MICHAEL: Thank you.

KAREN: I thought we might go for a walk. It's a lovely night. We could have the wine on the beach.

MICHAEL: Sorry. My best and oldest buddy is in from Toronto. He'll be back any second.

KAREN: Oh. Well then . . . I hope my behaviour this afternoon . . .

MICHAEL: No. No. It's not that.

KAREN: Really Michael. I don't know what came over me.

MICHAEL: I don't think now's the time to talk about it. Let's give it a few days.

KAREN: To become so anxiety ridden and uptight and unresponsive at such a time. Well. It couldn't have been much fun for you. I owe you an apology.

MICHAEL: You're making far too much of it.

KAREN: *(some intensity)* Don't demean me by making light of it.

MICHAEL: Right. Sorry.

KAREN: I've always hated the kind of woman who behaves that way. I hope you don't think that I'm the kind of woman who's incapable of having a casual affair with a good friend.

MICHAEL: I don't think that Karen. I know that you're capable of having a casual affair with just about any man you set mind to.

KAREN: Yes. And having a hell of a good time while I'm at it.

MICHAEL: Well then. That goes without saying, doesn't it?

They smile at their nonsense.

KAREN: I guess I was feeling a little guilty.

MICHAEL: Well. Sometimes it gets the better of us.

KAREN: It's a disgusting emotion. And there's absolutely no place for it in this situation. Michael I've thought about my behaviour this afternoon. I understand it. Both emotionally and intellectually. I really have come to grips with it. And I can assure you that that kind of neurotic episode can never happen again.

MICHAEL: Good. Then the afternoon wasn't a complete waste of time. I didn't mean that, Karen. What I meant was that when people are friendly with each other and like each other and are curious about each other well, then, sometimes they do things to each other that maybe they should do only to others.

KAREN: I'm not looking for an intense emotional involvement. What I have in mind is a very casual, very informal, adult affair. No demands. No responsibilities. Just good clean fun. Nothing will change between us Michael. Nothing. Except that we'll sleep together on a regular basis.

MICHAEL: Karen I'm sure you're aware that people sometimes convince themselves they feel one thing when really they feel something completely different. And then sometimes we blow things up out of all proportion because, perhaps, we're reacting to the past. Danny, Melvin the flying dentist. So I think it would be best if we waited a few days to find out how we really feel. Okay?

KAREN: Okay.

MICHAEL: I'll call you Monday.

KAREN: Okay. Just think about it Michael. That's all I ask.

JACKIE *enters from the bathroom.*

JACKIE: Michael I'm seeing Jeffrey on Thursday. Why don't I . . .

KAREN: What do you do Michael? Give out lottery tickets as door prizes? Give every tenth woman a free pair of panty hose?

MICHAEL: Jackie and I met this evening under the most unusual circumstances. Jackie was at a party down the hall.

JACKIE: At Jim Loadman's? He's a foreman at The Alberta Wheat Pool. But most people know him as a shortstop. In the Industrial League? Last year he was voted most valuable player.

KAREN: You must keep track. How do you do it? Steal the labels from their panties and display them, mounted like butterflies, in a large red album.

MICHAEL: Jackie has a terrible problem with her back. There was no place to lie down at the party.

JACKIE: Wall-to-wall people.

MICHAEL: So I let her use the floor.

KAREN: Christ!

KAREN *turns away.* MICHAEL *throws* JACKIE *a look.* JACKIE *enters the bedroom.*

MICHAEL: *(to* KAREN*'s back)* Karen listen . . .

KAREN: *(turning)* There are so few decent men around these days. They're all fags or running around after eighteen-year-olds.

MICHAEL: I'm sure you haven't exhausted all the men in the city.

KAREN: Michael you are so damn blind about everything. I've been screwing myself silly for months. Christ if something good doesn't happen soon I'll start making it with my students. Michael I know you. I understand you. It'll work. I know it will. God damn you Michael. Why do I have to demean myself like this in front of you?

MICHAEL: I'm sorry. I didn't know you felt this way. Or maybe and I did and conveniently ignored it. You were free. I was free. At the time there seemed no reason no to. It was a mistake Karen. Let's not make it worse.

KAREN *walks to the door. She turns.*

KAREN: By the way Michael. Have you ever met Earl? He's one of the most dynamic, charming, attractive, tall, broad shoulders, smouldering dark eyes men I have ever had the pleasure of being in the same room with. What is it about men of that age? They have a drive, a freshness, an energy, that men lose when they hit thirty.

MICHAEL: It's called 'naïveté' and they're well rid of it.

KAREN: I think he's putting it to your girl friend. It's the first intelligent thing Beth has done since you moved out. Face it Michael. It's over between you two.

MICHAEL: I hurt you. Now you hurt me.

KAREN: That's about it.

DAVE *enters.*

DAVE: *(to* KAREN*)* Hello.

KAREN: Hello. Good-bye.

KAREN *leaves.*

DAVE: Who was that?

MICHAEL: Karen Sperling. How's Beth?

DAVE: I don't know. Karen Sperling. What does she do?

MICHAEL: She teaches English at the university. What do you mean you don't know?

DAVE: I mean I don't know.

MICHAEL: Did she get going all right?

DAVE: Yeah. Maybe her choke is sticking. Maybe her carburetor is lousy. Don't ask me about cars.

DAVE *enters the kitchen to get a paper towel for his hands.*

MICHAEL: But you saw her drive away?

DAVE: *(off)* Yes.

MICHAEL: Did she say where she was going?

DAVE: *(off)* This Earl fella. He's throwing a party.

MICHAEL: Oh.

MICHAEL *walks to the bar, pours himself a scotch.* DAVE *enters from the kitchen wiping at his hands with a paper towel.*

DAVE: I know it's none of my business Mike. But do you know what you're doing?

MICHAEL: I know what I'm doing. I know exactly what I'm doing. I don't know what the hell I'm doing. What am I doing?

DAVE: *(getting rid of his paper towel in the wastepaper basket)* Jeez Mike. I don't know what to say. I haven't been single for eight years but I know how it must be. Look. If you want to get married and have kids, that's fine with me. And if you want to put an ad in the paper and make it with three bald women and a fox terrier twice a day, that's also fine with me. Because you see Mike, I'm your friend and whatever you do I'll understand and I'll never judge and I'll never advise and you're all on your own. Doesn't help much does it best buddy? Where's the lady with the backbone.

MICHAEL: In the bedroom.

DAVE: *(mocking)* Joseph Stalin. Do you know him? He's a Russian dictator but he has a marvelous sense of humour. The mountains and the vistas and the natural grandeur. I don't believe a word of it. It's all bullshit. I usually eat there on Wednesdays. I have the section near the windows. I'll look for you.

MICHAEL: I thought you were just horsing around. I didn't think you were serious.

DAVE: You didn't?

MICHAEL: No. . Well. . Maybe I did. I don't know. I guess I just wasn't thinking. You know how you are with strange women. It was obvious you weren't going to get anything from her. I don't know Dave, it felt like ten years ago and I guess I did what I always did. I'm sorry.

DAVE: Yeah?

MICHAEL: Dave. I mean it.

DAVE: *(getting his jacket)* Too fucking late.

MICHAEL: Where are you going?

DAVE: To that party. Stalin's friend was strike one. I'm told I get three.

MICHAEL: Dave. Think about it.

DAVE: Eight years Mike. Eight years is a long time. Eight years is no joke.

DAVE *walks to the door.*

MICHAEL: Okay Dave. Go on. You deserve it. You're a successful lawyer. You've put in your time. It's coming to you. Go ahead. Join the Liberal Party and get your piece of ass.

DAVE: I don't know where you get off talking to me like this. We're no different you and me. Just because you don't say tits and ass, just because you say arrangement, just because you talk freedom and growth rather than getting laid, just because you're full up to here with all this crap of sexual chic doesn't mean you're not just another horny guy looking to get fucked.

MICHAEL: I know that Dave. Okay? All I'm saying is that acting on it doesn't make it any better.

DAVE: And you know something else. Being up front about your failings doesn't make them any better. When you've got B.O. you've got B.O. The solution is not to tell your girlfriend you smell bad and you want an arrangement. The solution is to take a god damn bath. Jesus Christ Mike, you're driving Beth crazy.

MICHAEL: Yeah.

DAVE *moves to the door.* MICHAEL *cuts him off.*

MICHAEL: I'm telling you. Don't be an idiot.

DAVE: You haven't been doing without. I have. I haven't had any of it. And I'm going to get some of it. Even if it damn well kills me.

MICHAEL: It's exciting and romantic. It's one hell of a rush. I'm not going to deny that. But getting laid is not a detachable event. Acts have consequences and they're never the ones you want or the ones you expect. Dave. Just take it from me. It's not worth it.

DAVE: Thanks for the sermon. I'll keep it in mind.

DAVE *moves to the door.* MICHAEL, *trying to lighten things up, good naturedly gets* DAVE *in a headlock.*

MICHAEL: Dave please. Don't make me tie you up.

DAVE: *(intensely)* Let go.

MICHAEL *releases* DAVE. DAVE *walks to the door.*

MICHAEL: I'll see you tomorrow?

DAVE *says nothing and leaves. There is a short pause.* MICHAEL *hurries to the desk, looks up a number in the phone book and dials.*

MICHAEL: Hello. . Who am I talking to please? Ah. . Listen. . Ah you don't know me Earl, but we have a mutual friend. Beth Gordon. . That's right. It's Michael Kaye. . Yes. And I've heard a lot about you. Is Beth there?. . Well it could be car trouble. . It's not your fault. No one's to blame for a lemon. Could you have Beth call me when she arrives?. . Oh. . Good. Sure I'll hang on. . Beth. Mike. . I want to talk to you. What do you think I want?. . No it couldn't wait. It's important. . Yes I know where you are. Do you think this is easy for me?. . I want to talk to you. I thought you were the one who was sick of all this. . *(*BETH *has hung up)* Beth? Beth? *(slamming down the phone)* Fuck!

MICHAEL *turns away from the desk, then, after a moment, he takes his jacket from the closet, and goes to the desk and marks down Earl's address.* JACKIE *enters from the bedroom.*

JACKIE: Did everyone leave?

MICHAEL: *(startled by* JACKIE*)* Oh my God . . Not everyone. I was just on my way out.

JACKIE: Michael this wonderful thing happened. I was trying to get comfortable on your bedroom floor when suddenly something in my back popped. I feel just terrific.

MICHAEL: Jackie. The time has come for you to quietly fold your little tent and leave my apartment.

JACKIE: You look very tense and anxious.

MICHAEL: I am.

JACKIE: I know just the thing.

JACKIE *approaches* MICHAEL *and attempts to give him a back-rub.* MICHAEL *moves away.*

MICHAEL: Just what do you think you are doing?

JACKIE: You'll feel like a new man. I promise.

JACKIE *tries again.*

MICHAEL: Jackie!

Short pause.

JACKIE: I thought you were interested.

MICHAEL: I was.

JACKIE: What happened? Was it something I said? I talk too much. I know I talk too much.

MICHAEL: It's not that. Why is it you don't want to leave this apartment?

There is a loud knock on the door.

JACKIE: That's why.

JACKIE *goes to the door and looks through the peep hole. There is another loud knock.*

MICHAEL: Who's that?

JACKIE: Phil.

JACKIE *slips the chain and locks the door. There is another knock.*

JACKIE: He's a big dumb jock and he's very drunk.

The door is shaken violently. JACKIE *moves away from the door.*

MICHAEL: What does he want?

JACKIE: He's my husband. He thinks we're screwing. He wants to beat the piss out of you.

The shaking continues. The door frame gives way.

BLACKOUT

Scene III

Sunday morning, 11:30.

KAREN *and* DAVE *are sitting on the couch. Their arms are around each other.*

DAVE: I was thinking body oils. Rose, lavender, peach blossom. I cover you in it. Then I sniff you all over. Then you cover me in it. Then you sniff me all over.

KAREN: I was thinking hot tubs. We can watch the water gurgle.

DAVE: Then there's always leather.

KAREN: I have just the thing. It's not leather but it'll do. An old fashioned corset. It cinches up. No bottom half. Black garter belts.

DAVE: Actually I was thinking leather thongs.

KAREN: David.

DAVE: I'm enlightened. I tie you up. Then you tie me up.

KAREN: You're crazy.

DAVE: A movie. Starring you. And me. It begins. You're naked. Covered in oil. Tied to the bed with leather thongs. I enter. Also naked. But not covered in oil. I look at your naked, oiled, tied up body. I give a fiendish ha ha. Ha ha. I turn my back to look at the other five women in the room.

KAREN: Well excuse me.

DAVE: But you're hot and sweaty and the oil has loosened the thongs. You squirm free and quick as a wink, while my back is turned, you overpower me.

KAREN: Good for me.

DAVE: Wait a minute. You're no better than me. You're just as twisted. You bind me with leather, douse me in oil, peach blossom, and then, with one of your perverse giggles . .

KAREN: *(a giggle)*

DAVE: . . . you sadistically sniff me all over.

KAREN: Oooh . . Then.

DAVE: Then?

KAREN: *(standing up)* Your body a quivering mass on the floor I leave.

DAVE: You leave?

KAREN: I leave. But I return in a moment clad in my crotchless corset.

DAVE: Vunderbar!

KAREN: And carrying a twelve-foot bull whip.

DAVE: Oh my God!

KAREN: But by this time you have slithered free.

DAVE: *(standing up)* Slither, slither. I grab the whip from your oily hand and raise it above my head.

KAREN: When suddenly you catch sight of my liquid pools.

DAVE: Liquid pools?

KAREN: Eyes.

DAVE: Ah.

KAREN: We embrace passionately and make convulsive oily love.

DAVE: All over the bedroom floor. We don't worry about the wall-to-wall.

KAREN: What do we care. It's just some sleazy motel.

DAVE: Then I order in some beer and pizza and the two of us, content and happy, watch the last two periods between the Leafs and the Canadiens.

KAREN: Let's go. Sex fiend.

DAVE: Let's wait another five minutes.

KAREN: You left him a note. You'll call him this afternoon.

DAVE: Five minutes. It's important. I may not see him for another year. I still don't like the looks of that door. And all this dirt.

KAREN: An accident.

DAVE: Could be. I'll have another look around.

DAVE *enters the dining room.*

KAREN: *(looking around, to herself)* Where is my purse?

DAVE: *(off)* Oh my God!

KAREN: David! David!

DAVE *returns with the remains of the bonsai.*

DAVE: The bonsai is no more.

KAREN: You scared me half to death.

DAVE: Bad joke. Sorry sweetie.

DAVE *gives* KAREN *a kiss.* MICHAEL *enters.*

KAREN: Mike.

DAVE: Mike. How are you?

KAREN: What is wrong with your eye?

MICHAEL: It's nothing.

DAVE: What do you mean nothing. That's a beaut.

KAREN: What happened?

MICHAEL: Last night this big guy breaks down the door, knocks over my bonsai and punches me in the face. I got in a good one though. Adam's apple. He was a nice deep blue here for five minutes. I was at emergency until three waiting to get sewn up. I really don't want to talk about it. What are you two doing here?

DAVE: I just dropped in to say goodbye.

KAREN: We've been trying to phone you all morning.

DAVE: There was no answer

KAREN: We've been knocking on your door.

DAVE: There was no answer.

KAREN: But the door was unlocked.

DAVE: So we just walked in . . . Karen and I. Met.

KAREN: Actually we've become quite good friends.

DAVE: Actually a little more than friends.

KAREN: Actually Dave's right.

DAVE: Life. Figure it out.

KAREN: People. Figure them out.

DAVE: That Vancouver guy. It was Earl. Imagine that.

KAREN: I remembered Dave from your apartment.

DAVE: Karen was the only person I knew. Next to the guys.

MICHAEL: Wasn't Beth there?

DAVE: Oh she was there. I just didn't see much of her. She was there for a second. Then she was gone.

KAREN: Just swallowed up by the crowd. Never to be seen again.

DAVE: So many people. All trying to get at each other. We hit it off right away. Everything happened so quickly.

KAREN: Thank God for that. We have so little time. Dave's leaving for Toronto first thing in the morning. We won't be able to spend any time together until he gets back from England.

MICHAEL: Oh. I didn't know you were going to England.

DAVE: I can't believe I didn't tell you. Four months. For the Federal Government. I wasn't supposed to tell anyone. Very hush-hush.

MICHAEL: What about your affairs in Toronto?

DAVE: No problem. I'll sublet my apartment and Bannerman will look after my practice.

MICHAEL: *(walking to the phone)* Well. Isn't that Bannerman one hell of a nice guy?

KAREN: We're going to spend two weeks together in September.

MICHAEL: Really? Two weeks?

DAVE: Yeah. Two weeks.

MICHAEL: Where are you going? Maui?

KAREN: Sooke. I know this lovely inn.

MICHAEL: Well. That sounds wonderful.

MICHAEL *dials.*

KAREN: We should go.

DAVE: What's your rush?

KAREN: I want to luxuriate over brunch.

DAVE: We have lots of time. I want to talk to Mike.

KAREN: Have you seen my purse?

DAVE: Don't worry sweetie. It's around.

MICHAEL *hangs up the phone.*

MICHAEL: It's not like Beth to disappear on a Sunday morning.

KAREN: Have you tried Earl's?

MICHAEL *glares at* KAREN.

DAVE: Stop worrying. She'll turn up.

MICHAEL: I've been trying to get in touch with her all morning.

KAREN: *(remembering)* She's playing tennis.

MICHAEL: What?

KAREN: We had a tennis lesson this morning.

MICHAEL: How long does it go?

KAREN: She'll be another hour at least.

DAVE: Well then. Let's have some coffee with Mike. Mike?

MICHAEL: Uh. Sure.

KAREN: What about our brunch?

DAVE: It's happening. We'll just visit for a little while. Karen please.

KAREN: I'll put the kettle on.

DAVE: Thanks sweetie. You get things started. I'll finish things off.

DAVE *gives* KAREN *a domestic little kiss.*

MICHAEL: There should be some apple strudel in the fridge if you want to warm it up.

KAREN: I'll find it.

KAREN *leaves.*

DAVE: Well? What do you think?

MICHAEL: Huh? About what?

DAVE: Jesus Christ Mike, this is the morning after the night before. This is the first time in eight years that I've got a night before to talk about. I'm enjoying this. Talking about it. It's exciting just talking about talking about it. Aren't you even happy for me?

MICHAEL: I hope you had a nice time.

DAVE: Ferocious. Absolutely ferocious.

MICHAEL: Ferocious?

DAVE: Did you ever go to bed with a member of the English department? Do it. I recommend it wholeheartedly. I don't want to tell tales out of school but, a wild, impetuous, passionate night. And after eight years of married life I was ready for it.

KAREN: *(off)* I need a pan for the strudel.

MICHAEL: Under the stove.

DAVE: Have you known Karen for a long time?

MICHAEL: Three, four years.

DAVE: She's a good friend?

MICHAEL: Pretty good.

DAVE: She always like this?

MICHAEL: Like what?

DAVE: No hassle, exciting, fun, good times.

MICHAEL: I guess.

DAVE: Nice girl.

MICHAEL: Dave.

DAVE: Yeah.

MICHAEL: Sooke?

DAVE: We had a great time. We really got along . . . Christ I don't know.

KAREN *sticks her head into the living room.*

KAREN: David could you give me a hand with the coffee?

DAVE: Sure sweetie. *(as* KAREN *disappears from view)* I don't know Mike. I just don't know.

DAVE *enters the kitchen. Giggles and laughter from the kitchen.*

KAREN: *(off)* Stop that David. We have to make the coffee.

KAREN *enters with just the cream.*

KAREN: It's not as bad or as simple as it seems. I'll admit that last night I was angry and vindictive and the only reason I came on to David in the first place was to get back at you.

DAVE: *(off)* Where's the coffee?

MICHAEL: In the fridge.

KAREN: I never thought he'd turn out to be such a sweet, nice man. I never thought I'd have such a wonderful time.

DAVE: *(off)* Found it.

KAREN: I wasn't expecting it. I wasn't expecting that I was doing what I was doing. It started out one way but it ended up another.

DAVE: *(off)* This coffee is going to win me a golden cup.

KAREN: Yesterday afternoon. I was desperate. I made a mistake. It's best forgotten. No one need ever know anything.

MICHAEL: I haven't had time to think about it.

KAREN: You're doing very well.

MICHAEL: What if something comes up?

KAREN: Lie.

MICHAEL *shakes his head.*

KAREN: You should never have gone to bed with me in the first place if you weren't willing to lie about it.

MICHAEL: Karen, I should never have gone to bed with you period.

DAVE: *(off)* Should I cut up the strudel before I heat it up?

KAREN: *(calling)* No.

DAVE: *(off)* Three-fifty?

KAREN: *(calling)* I'll be there in a second. *(to* MICHAEL*)* Michael you're gracious and honest and well intentioned and you don't talk dirty and it doesn't mean one damn thing. If you cause pain you cause pain and all the heartfelt talk in the world doesn't make one bit of difference.

DAVE: *(off)* Tin foil?

KAREN: Coming.

KAREN *enters the kitchen. There is a knock on the door.* MICHAEL *answers it.* BETH *is there.*

MICHAEL: Beth. C'mon in.

BETH: Mike what happened to your eye?

MICHAEL: It's nothing.

BETH: Let me see.

MICHAEL: It's nothing. Really.

BETH: What happened?

MICHAEL: I'll tell you all about it later. Sit down. Please. I've been trying to get in touch with you all morning.

BETH: I went for a walk. It's such a beautiful morning.

MICHAEL: How was it?

BETH: Oh it did the trick. Mike, we have to talk.

KAREN *enters with plates and silverware on a tray.*

KAREN: Michael do you have any cinammon? *(noticing* BETH*)* Beth.

BETH: Hi Karen. I didn't know you were here.

KAREN: Just getting some coffe and pastry together.

BETH: I see.

KAREN: You didn't go to tennis?

BETH: No. Neither did you.

KAREN: Sunday mornings.

BETH: Yes.

KAREN: Great party last night. I felt like a kid again.

BETH: We weren't expecting that many people.

KAREN: Oh no. I liked the crush. I was putting coffee on. But maybe you and Michael. . .

BETH: Don't leave on my account. Perhaps I'm the one who should go?

KAREN: No, no, no. Michael's been trying to get in touch with you all morning.

BETH: Really?

KAREN: Yes. Oh silly you. I was just on my way to an absolutely decadent brunch. I only dropped in for a moment. Not five minutes ago. With an old friend of Michael's. He's an absolutely wonderful man. we just popped round to say goodbye. The mad fool has to go to England for four months. *(calling)* David. We've had a marvellous, glorious twelve hours. I'm still reeling. *(calling)* David. There's someone who wants to say hello. *(KAREN sticks her head into the kitchen looking for DAVE. DAVE enters from the dining room with a forced smile on his face.)* Ah there you are. I think you two know each other.

DAVE: Hi Beth.

BETH: Dave.

DAVE: Old friends.

MICHAEL: Can you believe it? Dave's going to England for four months. These bachelor lawyers. The world's their oyster.

BETH: Well I hope Dave doesn't get indigestion.

DAVE: Ha ha. The job's in London. For the Federal Government. Very hush-hush.

BETH: That's all right Dave. I can keep a secret.

KAREN: David's flying back here when he returns from England. We're going to spend two weeks in Sooke.

BETH: Very romantic. You'll be a very busy man these next four months.

DAVE: You know me. Pressure. I thrive on it.

KAREN: Beth. Coffee? *(without allowing* BETH *to respond)* Another cup, serviettes, oh my God, the strudel.

KAREN *exits to the kitchen.*

DAVE: Thanks.

BETH: You're out of your mind.

DAVE: Yeah. Well. Only in B.C. And I've made my peace with it.

DAVE *exits to the kitchen.*

MICHAEL: I tried but he's an adult.

BETH: I doubt it.

MICHAEL: Beth.

BETH: I'd like to apologize for that phone call.

MICHAEL: Forget it.

BETH: And for how I behaved last night.

MICHAEL: Someone hurts you. You hurt them back. It's human nature.

BETH: Yes. We've done a lot of that. I think we should call it quits.

MICHAEL: What? . . Why? Earl?

BETH: No Michael.

MICHAEL: Why then?

BETH: How can you ask me that? I want it all. A husband, a family, a home for my family. The whole banal, bourgeois package. That's what I want. That's who I am. So let's just forget the whole damn thing because I'm not going to let you or anyone else make me feel guilty about it any longer.

MICHAEL: Beth listen . . .

BETH: No. Let me finish. When you started talking 'arrangement' I should have told you to get lost. But I was too scared. Of losing you. Of being out in that meat market looking for a man. Jesus Christ I'm thirty. What if I didn't meet someone for a while. And even if I did I'm not going to get married and have kids with someone I just met. And god damn it Mike. I was hoping you'd come through.

MICHAEL: And I have come through. That's what I've been trying to tell you. Beth. You're very special to me. I love you very much.

BETH: And I resent the hell out of you. Sometimes I don't even like you. God knows I don't respect you the way I used to. And there's no sense in even talking about trust.

MICHAEL: The arrangement was a big mistake. I know that now. But we can get over it.

BETH: These last few months. They're not marks on paper. They're here. With us.

KAREN *enters with the strudel.*

KAREN: Here's the strudel. And I found some melon. *(noticing the tension)* Why don't I cut this in the kitchen?

KAREN *returns to the kitchen.*

MICHAEL: *(now deciding not to tell* BETH *about* KAREN*)* I've been a big jerk. But that's over with. History. It's best forgotten. Beth? Let's give it another chance.

BETH: It's not that I've stopped caring about you.

MICHAEL: There's more to us than these last few months.

BETH: I know that.

MICHAEL: We can do it. I've got all this garbage out of my system.

BETH: Mike it doesn't work that way. Why are you doing this to me?

MICHAEL: We'll get it straight. You'll see.

BETH: Mike please.

MICHAEL: All right then. We'll have dinner tonight. We'll go to that nice little Portugese place you like so much.

BETH: No.

MICHAEL: Tomorrow then? Beth? Please.

BETH: Okay Mike. We'll talk.

DAVE *enters with a pot of coffee.* KAREN *follows with the strudel and melon.*

KAREN: Here we go. David will pour the coffee. This is an absolutely perfect melon. Did you pick this Michael?

MICHAEL: Uh-huh.

KAREN: Well you certainly have a way with fruit. I go crazy in produce sections. I don't know whether to pinch of prod or sniff or squeeze.

DAVE: Sniff?

KAREN: Pineapples.

DAVE: Yeah? You sure? Where do you sniff them?

KAREN: All over David. Where do you think?

BETH: Just the top.

BETH hands MICHAEL his coffee. KAREN offers DAVE some melon.

DAVE: None for me. I'll stick to strudel. Carbohydrates. They keep you young.

KAREN: And ruin your appetite. We are going for brunch. It's melon or nothing. Wonderful coffee.

DAVE: I told you. *(takes a sip)* Delish. *(takes another sip)* Delish, delish, delish. A little time, a little effort. And God rewards.

KAREN: You're not hungry?

BETH: Coffee first.

KAREN: Oh.

MICHAEL: To wake up the system. Quite the spread you put on Karen. Thank you.

KAREN: David warmed the strudel.

DAVE: And cut the melon. And got the plates. And made the coffee. Delish, delish, delish.

There is a knock on the door. MICHAEL answers it. JACKIE is there. She bursts into the apartment. She is carrying two small pieces of luggage.

JACKIE: Free at last Michael. Free at last. Oh. Does that eye hurt?

MICHAEL: It's fine.

JACKIE: I'm sorry. I didn't know you had people over. Hello David.

DAVE: Hi.

JACKIE: I just came by to say I'm sorry. And Phil's sorry too. He's swallowing now.

MICHAEL: Good.

JACKIE: Here's a cheque for fifty dollars. For the door.

MICHAEL: I can't take this.

JACKIE: Please. It'll make Phil feel better.

MICHAEL: *(taking the cheque)* Thanks.

JACKIE: I've made my decision. I'm leaving Phil. *(to the group at large)* Phil's my husband.

KAREN: And he mangled the door?

JACKIE: Yes.

BETH: And hit Michael?

JACKIE: Yes.

BETH: Why?

JACKIE: Jeffrey Fiskin thinks it's Burnaby but I think . . .

MICHAEL: *(cutting* JACKIE *off)* I'll tell you all about it later. Nice seeing you again Jackie.

BETH: Mike why are you being so rude? Do you want some coffee Jackie?

JACKIE: *(walking to the couch)* No thanks. Someone's supposed to be picking me up out front. Anyway Jeffrey's diagnosis is Burnaby but I think Jeffrey is full of it. *(sitting down)* Jeffrey's my psychiatrist. Very eclectic. I've been puking for months. Jeffrey blames it all on Burnaby. But I knew it couldn't just be Burnaby. I knew it was also Phil LeMieux. Phil and I got married just out of high school but we've been drifting apart since I started throwing up. I've been dancing and painting and meeting all these interesting people. And Phil, well, he's been working at the Wheat Pool and going through a dozen Blues a night and playing baseball like a maniac. Just generally being your basic veg. Last night at Jim's. Jim Loadman? Phil's foreman at the Pool. Well I told Phil I wanted the freedom to experiment. We had this big fight and my back started to act up. And then I met Michael and David. Nothing happened. But Phil didn't know that. I've been in Burnaby arguing all night. I realize now that Phil is a very little person and that some people just can't handle change. He resents and he won't forgive. Well I'm bigger than that. This is all I took. And it feels just great. That's what I was thinking when I walked in. Goodbye Burnaby. Goodby Maalox. Free at last Michael. Free at last. *(getting up and walking to* MICHAEL*)* I'm sorry you had to be a part of all this.

Moving JACKIE *to the door.*

MICHAEL: It's all water under the bridge.

JACKIE: *(returning to the couch)* Guess I better be going. Bernard's picking me up out front. He always gets lost in Burnaby. Besides I didn't want him to run into Phil. *(sitting down)* Bernard Hedley, he's been painting for over forty years, kind of a mentor figure for me. Well, I'm moving in. He's got this boat, close to forty feet, in a month he's going to sail the inside passage to Alaska. I'll be his deck hand.

DAVE: Bon voyage Jackie.

JACKIE: I guess I owe you an apology too David. I wasn't straight with you either.

DAVE: Forget it.

MICHAEL: *(hurrying* JACKIE *to the door)* You should wait for Bernard out front.

DAVE: Mentor figures are very impatient.

MICHAEL: Forty years waiting for a protégé like you. He must be getting antsy.

JACKIE: *(turning to* DAVE*)* I just want you to know I respect you.

DAVE: Thanks. See yuh.

MICHAEL: Bye-bye Jackie

JACKIE: *(walking to* DAVE*)* You were honest about your wife in Toronto. I should have been as honest about Phil down the hall.

DAVE: Shit.

KAREN: Wife?

JACKIE: And family. Three boys.

KAREN: Where is my god damn purse?

DAVE: Karen don't be like that.

KAREN: Why didn't you have the guts to tell me the truth?

DAVE: *(following* KAREN *around in her search for her purse)* Some women don't like to get involved with married men.

KAREN: I don't give a damn about your marital status. I hate being lied to.

DAVE: I'm new to all this.

KAREN: Well then that makes everything just fine.

DAVE: I thought it would make things easier.

KAREN: You all knew, didn't you? Lovely. Just dandy. I love being treated this way. It does wonders for my self-esteem. And what's all this crap about two weeks away from it all?

DAVE: I'm serious. I'm looking forward to it.

KAREN: *(pushing past* DAVE *into the dining room in her search for her purse.)* Bring your wife and kids. We'll save money on the ferry.

KAREN *enters the dining room.*

DAVE: *(following* KAREN *into the dining room)* I'll work something out. I promise.

KAREN: *(off, from the dining room)* Forget it David. I don't need you. There are twelve nineteen-year-olds in my first-year section who would like nothing better than to tie me up and douse me in oil. Where is my god damn purse?

JACKIE: *(hurrying to sit down, a loud moan, a hand to her stomach)*

KAREN *enters from the dining room.* DAVE *follows.* KAREN *continues her frantic search for her purse.*

DAVE: Karen. Can't we handle this in a civilized manner? Let's talk about it. We'll go to the Four Seasons. We'll have that brunch.

JACKIE: Don't go there. You'll never get in.

DAVE: Sure we will.

JACKIE: Not today. The place will be just packed.

DAVE: So we'll go someplace else. Now get lost!

BETH: Dave. Unless you have reservations I'd forget about brunch.

DAVE: What is so special about . . . Oh shit!

MICHAEL: What is it?

JACKIE: It's Mother's Day.

KAREN: Charming. Absolutely charming. That would have made for a very interesting brunch. Why can't I find anything when I need it?

JACKIE: This is all my fault. I'm so sorry. I'm not stupid. I'm really very sensitive. It's because I never saw them as a couple. It didn't make sense to me. So I didn't know to be quiet.

MICHAEL: It's all right Jackie. It's not your fault.

JACKIE: But David you must understand. *(*DAVE *turns away from* JACKIE. JACKIE *turns to* MICHAEL.*)* When things make sense to me I'm really very perceptive. I'm very astute. When I saw you and her together. *(gesturing to* KAREN*)* I knew right away something had been cooking. Because you two make sense together. And that's another reason I got things . . . *(*JACKIE *trails off and sits down. Perhaps she clutches her stomach.)*

BETH: What kind of sense did you and Karen make together?

Short pause. KAREN *laughs loudly.*

KAREN: Last night Michael and I were having a disagreement over Milton. This mindless muffin walked in on it. She obviously took our heated discussion of *Paradise Lost* to be sexual recrimination.

Short pause.

KAREN: I really don't know how you can take this space cadet from Burnaby seriously.

BETH *looks at* MICHAEL. MICHAEL *turns away.*

KAREN: Michael you are such a fool.

MICHAEL: I didn't see any point in telling you.

BETH: When?

MICHAEL: Yesterday afternoon.

KAREN: The one and only time.

MICHAEL: We did something very stupid. It was a big mistake.

KAREN: I really can't understand just how or why it happened . .

Short pause. A long look between MICHAEL *and* BETH.

KAREN: It was just one of those things. It means nothing. It's best forgotten. We both had an absolutely miserable time.

BETH *turns and walks away from* KAREN *towards the dining room.* KAREN *follows.*

KAREN: You had that silly, fatuous arrangement. Beth? Oh damn it.

JACKIE: Does anyone have some Maalox?

MICHAEL *walks towards* BETH.

DAVE: You and Karen?

MICHAEL: Dave.

KAREN: *(a look at* DAVE*)* I'll leave without my purse. I'll walk. Hitchhike. I don't care. *(remembering)* Oh right.

KAREN *exits to the bathroom.*

JACKIE: I'll take Rolaids if that's all you've got.

DAVE: Shit. The first time in eight years of marriage and on Mother's Day for fuck's sake. You shoulda said no to me right from the start. That's what a friend would have done. That's what I needed to hear. You shouldn't have been such a sophisticated, with it, enlightened son-of-a-bitch.

KAREN: *(off, from bathroom)* I can't believe my luck. Three men in one weekend. *(as she enters with her purse)* I'm not down. I'm out. Maybe I should try women.

KAREN *walks to the door.*

DAVE: Ten years later and I'm still getting you castoffs. Eh best buddy? And for what? To feel like a big man. Like the successful lawyer.

KAREN: *(at door)* Excuse me David. I didn't quite hear that. What did you call me?

Short pause. DAVE *doesn't relent.*

DAVE: Forget it.

KAREN: *(moving away from the door)* Well David 'castoff' may very well be apt. But I think you should know that I found your conversation inane—delish, delish, delish. Your stature second rate—I don't know where you got the idea that women would forget about your height if your talked about your density. We're interested in men not precious metals. And your performance unusual to say the least. Sniff, sniff. I think you'd rather inhale than orgasm. The only reason I put up with all these failings was because I wanted to inflict some pain on a former friend who had recently, as you so aptly put it, cast me off. Bye-bye all.

KAREN *leaves. She slams the door.* DAVE *boils.* MICHAEL *walks to* DAVE, *puts his arm on his shoulder.*

MICHAEL: Dave.

DAVE: Fuck off!!

DAVE *pushes* MICHAEL *away.* MICHAEL *sprawls into the sofa.*

JACKIE: I think I have to puke.

JACKIE *runs to the bathroom.* BETH *walks towards* MICHAEL. MICHAEL *looks towards* DAVE. DAVE *says nothing and leaves.*

BETH: Are you all right?

MICHAEL: I'm fine.

BETH: You sure.

MICHAEL: Yes. I'm fine.

JACKIE *returns from the bathroom holding a large bottle of Maalox.*

JACKIE: And Jeffrey Fiskin kept saying it was Burnaby. It's an ulcer. It has to be. Oh. I'm sorry. I found this. Can I keep it? Well. Bernard must be waiting.

JACKIE *takes a swig from the bottle, puts it down and leaves. There is a short pause. Then* BETH *walks to the door.*

MICHAEL: Beth. I'm sorry.

BETH: Yes. I know.

BETH *leaves.* MICHAEL *sits for moment, forces himself to get up, takes a sip of his coffee and turns on the stereo. He returns to the couch.*

THE LIGHTS FADE

THE END

In the original production the music Michael plays on his stereo at the beginning of the play and at the end was *Too Bad* by Doug and the Slugs. In the play's final moments when Michael realizes just what he has put on and how the lyrics relate to his situation he returns to the stereo and quickly changes the cut. The play and the audience seemed to need the humour of this small moment. It allowed them to leave the theatre with a smile on their faces without compromising either the theme of the play or the character of Michael.

We also used other music from Doug and the Slugs album *Cognac and Bologna* as incidental music throughout the show. Again it seemed to help the production.

S.S.